DAY-TO-DAY
WITH
Kimberella
AND *Prince*
Ain't-So-Charmin'
MY Prince Was NEVER a Frog!

KIMBERLY A. WEIRES

WESTBOW
PRESS®
A DIVISION OF THOMAS NELSON
& ZONDERVAN

Scriptures taken from the Holy Bible, New International Version®, NIV®. Copyright © 1973, 1978, 1984, 2011 by Biblica, Inc.™ Used by permission of Zondervan. All rights reserved worldwide. www.zondervan.com The "NIV" and "New International Version" are trademarks registered in the United States Patent and Trademark Office by Biblica, Inc.™

WestBow Press books may be ordered through booksellers or by contacting:

WestBow Press
A Division of Thomas Nelson & Zondervan
1663 Liberty Drive
Bloomington, IN 47403
www.westbowpress.com
1 (866) 928-1240

Because of the dynamic nature of the Internet, any web addresses or links contained in this book may have changed since publication and may no longer be valid. The views expressed in this work are solely those of the author and do not necessarily reflect the views of the publisher, and the publisher hereby disclaims any responsibility for them.

Any people depicted in stock imagery provided by Thinkstock are models, and such images are being used for illustrative purposes only. Certain stock imagery © Thinkstock.

ISBN: 978-1-5127-8782-5 (sc)
ISBN: 978-1-5127-8783-2 (hc)
ISBN: 978-1-5127-8781-8 (e)

Library of Congress Control Number: 2017908264

Print information available on the last page.

WestBow Press rev. date: 6/20/2017

♥Dedication♥:

I would like to thank my personal Savior, Jesus Christ; my husband and best friend on this earth, Rodney; our children, Jacob (Sara) and Julie (Grant); our grandchildren, Mary, Elinor, Isabelle, Cole and Kate; and our family and friends for many wonderful memories and for future ones that will more than likely come.

"WHY DIDN'T YOU CARE?!"

"Why didn't you tell me about getting saved
to make my trip to Heaven more easily paved?"
This could be a question asked of you or I
when we meet our loved ones after they die.
We need to share the Gospel with one another –
a friend, a neighbor, a sister or a brother.
Once saved, they'll be raised when they hear the horn,
otherwise, a lot of good people will suffer and mourn.
They'll have a chance within the seven years of doom
to claim Jesus as Savior and live in His mansion's room.
Some people never heard the Gospel or don't understand –
it's not just *going* to church, it's being held in God's hand.
The reason that I wrote these daily poems for this book,
is to reach out to God's creation for all to take a look.
Having Jesus as our best friend is a God-given blessing –
pure joy to know we'll live forever with the Almighty King.
For forgiveness of sins, a prayer will only take a minute
for Jesus to come into their hearts and also the Holy Spirit.
Then they will know how to live the life of a true Christian
and we'll see them in Heaven: friends, neighbors and kin.
The last thing we'll want to hear, that'll be too much to bear:
is....."Why didn't you tell me?" "Why didn't you care?"

✝ **1 Peter 3:15 But in your hearts revere Christ as Lord. Always be prepared to give an answer to everyone who asks you to give the reason for the hope that you have.**

✝ **Romans 6:23 For the wages of sin is death, but the gift of God is eternal life in Christ Jesus our Lord.**

✝ **Matthew 24:36 "But about that day or hour no one knows, not even the angels in Heaven, nor the Son, but only the Father."**

TOPICS

Age of Earth Baptism
Bible is True Creation
Big Bang Theory Faith
Ten Commandments
Jesus Christ is Savior
Noah's Ark Dinosaurs
Eternity Heaven Global Warming Being a Christian God Exists
Prayer Racism Weather The Flood Animals Bugs Worshipping
Universe Macro Evolution Creator Intelligent Designer Eating
Reading God's Word Relationships Wisdom Migration Comets
Sin Plants Good Works Grand Canyon Niagara Falls Museums
Choices Abortion Ants
Giants Big Gap Theory
Gravity Health Family
Fire-Breathing Dragons
Fishing Hunting Dreams
Cubits Christmas Easter
Earthquakes Revelation
Sasquatch Nessie Antlers
Gases Gardening Ocean
Wooly Mammoths Love
Judging Others Behavior
Bodies Symbiosis Teeth
Water Barrier Taste Buds
Talents Gifts Tornadoes
Sun Moon Stars Rainbow
Babies Children Marriage
Pets Fear Worry Emotions
Worms Languages Snakes

(and much more!)

ABO   OR

A UT   H

N   THE   T

N   AU

Y   W

L   L   E

R   I   I

E   V   R

B   E   E

M   S   S

I WITH   HER

K HUSBAND, RODNEY,

IN DUBUQUE, IO WA

T	2				F	D	I
H		C			U	O	N
E	M	H			D	G	
Y	A	I	AND		G		H
	R	L	5	S	Y	L	E
H	R	D		D		I	A
A	I	R	G	I	T	V	V
V	E	E	R	K	H	E	E
E	D	N	AND		E	S	N

OTHER BOOKS PUBLISHED
BY WEIRES IN THIS SERIES
OF DEVOTIONALS INCLUDE:
"IF THE SHOE FITS...RUN!"
"STILL HAVIN' A BALL!"
"IS IT MIDNIGHT YET?!"
2014   2015   2016
AND SHE LIKES TO
THINK OUTSIDE
THE BOX (OF
CANDY)

ix

Kimberella and Prince Roderick try to live a 'normal' day-to-day life in Dubuque, Iowa, but sometimes they fail to do so (quite often, but who's keeping track.)

Prince Roderick grew up in the country, learned how to build houses, played in a family band since age eleven, hunted, fished and explored the outdoors. Kimberella lived in the city, took piano lessons, baked, knitted and never quite grew up.

As husband and wife, they learned to get along by building two houses, playing in bands and living in Kimberella's childhood home in the city. They also go hunting, fishing and camping together.

They raised a son and daughter who are both married and each have children of their own. Their dog, Fudgy, is the master of the house. Witty Kitty is a smart cat that makes appearances whenever the mood strikes him.

'Jack and The Old Folk Band' is a Christian group that consists of themselves along with their son and D.J. They will play your special request, you just may not recognize it as such.

One thing all of the characters have in common is that they are God-loving Christians who go about their lives the best way they can, using God's Holy Bible as their guide.

Kimberella hopes that after reading this book every day for a year, and hopefully for many years to come, you will pick up *your* Bible and read it to receive God's message for you to get through any situation that may arise.

This is the fourth book of the devotional series "Day-To-Day with Kimberella and Prince Ain't-So-Charmin' ". Other books published by Weires are: "If the Shoe Fits…..Run!" (2014); "Still Havin' a Ball!" (2015) and "Is It Midnight Yet?!" (2016). Quite a few stories are based on actual experiences. The Bible always has a verse or two to go along with any activity the Buckskins find themselves in.

Cast of Characters

 Kimberella – Main character; wife of Prince Roderick; mother to Jack and Jules; grandmother to Mary Lu, Izzy Ann, Lanore, Chew-Chew and Baby No-No; member of 'Jack and The Old Folk Band'; princess wannabe

 Prince Roderick – Main character; husband of Kimberella; father to Jack and Jules; grandfather to Mary Lu, Izzy Ann, Lanore, Chew-Chew and Baby No-No; member of 'Jack and The Old Folk Band'; master-of-the-castle wannabe

 Jack – Son of Kimberella and Prince Roderick; husband of Sara-Sara; father to Mary Lu and Lanore; brother to Jules; member of 'Jack and The Old Folk Band'

 Sara-Sara – Daughter-In-Law of Kimberella and Prince Roderick; wife of Jack; mother to Mary Lu and Lanore

 Mary Lu – Granddaughter of Kimberella and Prince Roderick; daughter of Jack and Sara-Sara; big sister to Lanore; cousin to Izzy Ann, Chew-Chew and Baby No-No

 Lanore – Granddaughter of Kimberella and Prince Roderick; daughter of Jack and Sara-Sara; little sister to Mary Lu; cousin to Izzy Ann, Chew-Chew and Baby No-No

Jules – Daughter of Kimberella and Prince Roderick; wife of The General; mother to Izzy Ann, Chew-Chew and Baby No-No; sister to Jack; hostess to Witty Kitty

 The General – Son-In-Law of Kimberella and Prince Roderick; husband of Jules; father to Izzy Ann, Chew-Chew and Baby No-No; host to Witty Kitty

 Izzy Ann – Granddaughter of Kimberella and Prince Roderick; daughter of Jules and The General; big sister to Chew-Chew and Baby No-No; cousin to Mary Lu and Lanore

 Chew-Chew – Grandson of Kimberella and Prince Roderick; son of Jules and The General; little brother to Izzy Ann and big brother to Baby No-No; cousin to Mary Lu and Lanore

 Baby No-No – Granddaughter of Kimberella and Prince Roderick; daughter of Jules and The General; little sister to Izzy Ann and Chew-Chew; cousin to Mary Lu and Lanore

 Fudgy – Old English Sheepdog; so-called pet of Kimberella and Prince Roderick; master-of-the-castle; cousin to Witty Kitty; obnoxious, yet adorable

 Witty Kitty – Smart cat of no particular breed; Jules' and The General's house guest whenever he decides to stop in; cousin to Fudgy; handsome and sassy

D.J. – Member of 'Jack and The Old Folk Band'; not related to the other band members, but still treated like family (why should *he* be any different?)

 Rochelle – Kimberella's co-worker at the *Chewy Gooey Chocolate Factory*; family friend of the Buckskins

 Buddy – Prince Roderick's hunting and fishing partner (when Kimberella is unavailable); family friend of the Buckskins

 Auntie K.T. – Relative of the Buckskins who lives out of state and likes to share her love of gardening with others

Given enough time, a frog will turn into a prince.

Kimberella hasn't believed *that* one ever since she was a little girl reading a fairy tale book, while eating her oatmeal in the breakfast nook. Mrs. Buckskin doesn't care how much time is given or how long the frog has on this earth for livin' – a frog is a frog and a man is a man and if *she* can move on.....*anyone* can!

4.6 billion years...

January ❶

(Day 1 of 366)

Let's see what the Bible📖 has to say:

✝ Isaiah 9:6 For to us a child is born, to us a son is given, and the government will be on His shoulders. And He will be called Wonderful Counselor, Mighty God, Everlasting Father, Prince of Peace.

**Jules and The General are amazed at God's Creation.
A baby is usually born with finger and toe nails,
eyebrows, hair on their head and finger prints –
this is where Evolution pales.
Imagine a head waiting to develop a body,
or a body there hoping for a few organs.
If turning from a frog into a prince is what to believe –
a fish would sink to the bottom from a lack of fins.
Let's face it folks, it takes faith to believe in Evolution.
It takes a Designer with intelligence to create this place.
Smell the roses with the nose God made for you -
and with His help, it's not on your knee, it's on your face.**

🐝 ☺

January ❷

(Day 2 of 366)

Let's see what the Bible has to say:

⊤ Colossians 1:16 For by Him all things were created: things in Heaven and on earth, visible and invisible, whether thrones or powers or rulers or authorities; all things were created by Him and for Him.

Baby No-No was watching a caterpillar
crawling on the flower garden's wall.
The baby wanted to pet it,
but the height was just too tall.
Izzy Ann put the furry thing into a jar,
Baby No-No threw in a stick,
Chew-Chew added some grass to eat,
Jules poked holes in the lid with a pick.
They watched the orange and black insect
cover itself with a sticky coat.
When spring came and they took off the lid,
the butterfly used the air to float.
"Explain how that all evolved,"
Jules said to The General one night.
"How could a furry worm with all those legs,
figure out how to change into a creature of flight?"

Ж

January ❸

(Day 3 of 366)

Let's see what the Bible has to say:

† 2 Corinthians 5:17 Therefore, if anyone is in Christ, he
is a new Creation; the old has gone, the new has come!

**Witty Kitty and Fudgy would *like* to think
that it's funny how a nut is encased inside of a shell.
The problem is two-fold for them, however –
they *can't* think and should *both* be encased as well.**

January ❹

(Day 4 of 366)

Let's see what the Bible has to say:

⌐ Genesis 43:11 Then their father Israel said to them, "If it must be, then do this: Put some of the best products of the land in your bags and take them down to the man as a gift – a little balm and a little honey, some spices and myrrh, some pistachio nuts and almonds."

Prince Roderick is not sure what gravity is made of,
but he's pretty sure it's some heavy-duty stuff.
God must have created a kind of invisible goo
and of course knew how to make just enough.
Too little gravity would make us like helium balloons,
too much of the stuff would squash us flat.
It's always amazing to Mr. Buckskin
that God is *always* forever and ever "All that"!

↕

January ❺
(Day 5 of 366)

Let's see what the Bible has to say:

⸸ Job 26:7 He spreads out the northern skies over empty space; He suspends the earth over nothing.

Mrs. Buckskin told her son, Jack,
to turn down the radio and stop humming.
This way he can hear God speak to him
if he meditates – the conversations will keep coming.
Some people say that God doesn't exist
or that He's so far away it doesn't matter.
He can be so close, in fact, live inside of you,
if you'll accept Jesus and turn down the chatter.

January ❻

(Day 6 of 366)

Let's see what the Bible📖 has to say:

✝ Psalm 119:15 I meditate on your precepts and consider your ways.

In her classroom, Sara-Sara lit a candle.
She wanted to teach her kids a lesson.
"How long was the taper burning?"
she asked and then they started guessin'.
"We need to know how tall it was
before the flame was ever started.
Also, what is the rate of burning
and the length of the wick that departed?"
She explained that this is also true
of trying to figure out the age of the universe.
Unless we were there when it was made –
instead of believing the Big Bang, we need to converse.

January ❼

(Day 7 of 366)

Let's see what the Bible📖 has to say:

✝ Psalm 18:28 You, O Lord, keep my lamp burning; my God turns my darkness into light.

If there is a "bad" day in Heaven,
D.J. thinks that it would still outweigh the best day here.
There probably aren't days at all,
which would involve time.
We'll throw away our watches and
never shed another tear.
Imagine the best smell your nose
had the pleasure of smelling
and the most beautiful scenery you ever saw.
The peaceful sound of waves crashing onto the seashore
and the most yummy Thanksgiving
dinner prepared by your ma.
Remember a special day that made
your heart melt like snow
and memories of a child, getting a
present that was bought.
If we could have all of those things happen at once,
maybe we can imagine a day in Heaven
– what a lovely thought!

☻   ☺

January ❽
(Day 8 of 366)

Let's see what the Bible has to say:

† Revelation 21:4 "He will wipe away every tear from their eyes. There will be no more death or mourning or crying or pain, for the old order of things has passed away."

Witty Kitty was taking a stroll on the beach
and he stumbled upon a warning sign.
It said not to disturb the sea turtles' nests
or there could be imprisonment or a fine.
"Now that's a fine kettle of fish!"
he thought to himself on his somber way,
"they'll punish people for moving a turtle egg,
but killing human babies by the millions is okay?"

January ❾
(Day 9 of 366)

Let's see what the Bible📖 has to say:

✝ Ecclesiastes 11:5 As you do not know the path of the wind, or how the body is formed in a mother's womb, so you cannot understand the work of God, the Maker of all things.

Why does Kimberella wear her hair long,
especially when it's lost its shine and is droll?
Maybe because of the woman who wiped Jesus' feet –
using her hair that wasn't short like a pad of steel wool.

(☺)

January ❶⓿
(Day 10 of 366)

Let's see what the Bible📖 has to say:

† John 12:3 Then Mary took about a pint of pure nard, an expensive perfume; she poured it on Jesus' feet and wiped His feet with her hair. And the house was filled with the fragrance of the perfume.

**If Rochelle were aboard Noah's ark,
she would have studied the lizard.
She could have been seen running all around,
until she wore out her sandals and her gizzard.
The lizard is hard to catch with your hands
and there are six thousand species of their peers.
These reptiles have many overlapping scales,
four feet and don't forget external ears.**

≈≈≈◻≈≈≈

January ❶❶

(Day 11 of 366)

Let's see what the Bible📖 has to say:

✝ Proverbs 30:28 A lizard can be caught with the hand, yet it is found in kings' palaces.

Fudgy and Witty Kitty visited their friend, Amigo,
who is a Spanish speaking dog that lives next door.
He doesn't *speak* Spanish, but *was* trained that way –
his new owners had to learn a couple of words or more.
When Kimberella went over to meet the new pooch,
Mr. Smith said that *her* two were down for a nappy.
Mrs. Buckskin asked, "What about *your* new pup?"
He replied, "He's taking a siesta, can't you see?"

🐈 🐕 🐈

January ❶❷
(Day 12 of 366)

Let's see what the Bible has to say:

† Acts 2:8 Then how is it that each of us hears them in his own native language?

Kimberella learned the hard way
when she ignored God's advice.
He told her to avoid chocolate one night
when her stomach didn't feel very nice.
She did for a while and quit eating tasty treats,
but slowly added it back into her life.
She ate it whenever the mood struck her
and if her mood was wacky, she suffered from strife.
The moral is to listen to God
in everything you do, say or think.
He is the One who created us
and knew us before we were little and pink.

January ❶❸

(Day 13 of 366)

Let's see what the Bible📖 has to say:

✝ Isaiah 44:2 This is what the Lord says – He who made you, who formed you in the womb, and who will help you: Do not be afraid, O Jacob, my servant, Jeshuran, whom I have chosen.

Chew-Chew awoke with a little cough,
so Jules used a thermometer to take his temperature.
She isn't someone who thinks the worst,
but called the doctor, just to make sure.
"There are so many illnesses," the doc said to her,
"they are also referred to as diseases."
She asked him the difference between a cold and flu
and he said it depends on the number of sneezes.
Jules made a chart that she kept on the fridge,
to mark down every time she blessed him.
When The General came home and saw the list,
he packed up a bag and headed for the gym.
After becoming a daddy for the third time,
there's one thing he learned, yes siree bub...
that no matter if the child is sick or not,
don't EVER get in between a mother and her cub!
God didn't talk about the microscope,
because way back when, it wasn't around,
however, he *did* tell people to cover their upper lip
to help keep *others* healthy and sound.

🌡

January ❶❹

(Day 14 of 366)

Let's see what the Bible📖 has to say:

† 2 Chronicles 16:12 In the thirty-ninth year of his reign Asa was afflicted with a disease in his feet. Though his disease was severe, even in his illness he did not seek help from the Lord, but only from physicians.

**Mary Lu was taught to pray
every night before she sleeps.
God knows what we need before we ask,
but pray anyway...for our souls He keeps.**

✝

January ❶❺

(Day 15 of 366)

Let's see what the Bible📖 has to say:

✝ Romans 8:26 In the same way, the Spirit helps us in our weakness. We do not know what we ought to pray for, but the Spirit Himself intercedes for us with groans that words cannot express.

**The General heard a good one
from a Christian comedian's show in town.
"People that talk about politics as being right or left,
should really be concerned about going up or down."**

← → 🎭 ↑↓

January ❶❻

(Day 16 of 366)

Let's see what the Bible📖 has to say:

✝ Romans 6:23 For the wages of sin is death, but the gift of God is eternal life in Christ Jesus our Lord.

Too many people have the fear of family,
co-workers, neighbors and friends.
Jack says who they *really* should fear
is the Almighty God, because upon Him we depend.
We're scared that someone may laugh at us
when we talk about going to church,
so some won't say a word about their faith
to avoid sitting alone in the world on their perch.

☺   🚶🚶🚶 🚶🚶🚶 🚶🚶🚶

January ❶❼
(Day 17 of 366)

Let's see what the Bible📖 has to say:

† Proverbs 1:7 The fear of the Lord is the beginning of
knowledge, but fools despise wisdom and discipline.

Auntie K.T. was tending her garden,
pondering about life in a manner that was subtle.
Maybe Heaven is way bigger than we'll ever imagine –
it's probably like an ocean, not the size of a puddle.
We need to think more about Heaven
and less about our time here on this earth.
Whatever has you troubled *now* can't compare
to the other side with joy, laughter and all around mirth!

January ❶❽

(Day 18 of 366)

Let's see what the Bible📖 has to say:

✝ Romans 8:18 I consider that our present sufferings are not worth comparing with the glory that will be revealed in us.

Jack wants to know how many of you
know what he knows.
That's a funny question when you don't know
what he's talking about.
When he read the Book of Genesis,
regarding the Flood of Noah,
he found actual dates that the event occurred,
so there *should* be no doubt.
On the seventeenth day of the second month,
flood gates opened from Heaven.
The seventeenth day of the seventh month,
the ark came to rest.
On the first day of the tenth month,
the tops of the mountains appeared.
The first day of the first month,
Noah saw the water dried up, at best.
On the twenty-seventh day of the second month,
the earth was completely dry.
So in a nutshell, the whole process
took about one year.
Jack thinks that's a long time
to keep track on a calendar,
but God was with Noah and his family,
so they had no reason for fear.

January ❶❾

(Day 19 of 366)

Let's see what the Bible📖 has to say:

✝ **Genesis 8:13** By the first day of the first month of Noah's six hundred and first year, the water had dried up from the earth. Noah then removed the covering from the ark and saw that the surface of the ground was dry.

Why do we have dreams at night?
Sometimes they can give a person an awful fright.
Fudgy will sometimes kick his leg about
or make a scary noise come out of his snout.
Whenever Kimberella hears someone yack
that while sleeping, all they see is black,
she wishes that she could trade places,
but then again...would she see different faces?

January **20**
(Day 20 of 366)

Let's see what the Bible has to say:

Ecclesiastes 5:7 Much dreaming and many words are meaningless. Therefore stand in awe of God.

When you ask Jesus to enter into your heart
and ask for forgiveness of your sins,
the Holy Spirit moves within you forever
and will raise you above the needles and pins.
It's the same Holy Spirit that raised Jesus to Heaven
and He's powerful and a great comfort.
Rochelle says, "So no matter what your problems,
He'll be on your side of the net on any court!"

♥

January ❷❶

(Day 21 of 366)

Let's see what the Bible has to say:

⸸ Acts 2:38 Peter replied, "Repent and be baptized, every one of you, in the name of Jesus Christ for the forgiveness of your sins. And you will receive the gift of the Holy Spirit."

Prince Roderick would like to argue the fact
that macro Evolution ever occurred.
There's no empirical evidence to show
that a tomato plant turned into a flying bird.
There is, however, evidence of a rabbit's hair
being thicker in a colder terrain –
than a bunny's hair who lives in Florida,
when instead of snow, there is rain.

January ❷❷
(Day 22 of 366)

Let's see what the Bible📖 has to say:

✝ Leviticus 11:6 The rabbit, though it chews the cud, does not have a split hoof; it is unclean for you.

Today when Izzy Ann read her Bible,
it talked about morals.
She knows a little something about them
from her array of books.
One of the best ways
she will keep herself in line when older,
is to hang around people who love God
and stay away from the crooks.

January ❷❸
(Day 23 of 366)

Let's see what the Bible📖 has to say:

⊤ **1** Corinthians 15:33 Do not be misled: "Bad company corrupts good character."

Fly away birdy, fly away bird.
Where are you going, you creature of flight?
Are you going for the winter to somewhere warm?
Or will you return home sometime during the night?
Jules knows that birds who migrate
had to have help from God to do so.
Otherwise, they would just fly the coop
and not look back as they get up and go.

January ②④

(Day 24 of 366)

Let's see what the Bible📖 has to say:

✝ Proverbs 27:8 Like a bird that strays from its nest is a man who strays from his home.

Jack was explaining the five senses
to his daughters, Mary Lu and Lanore.
He had them smelling flowers with their noses
and feeling thorns with their thumbs and other four.
They tasted the apple that he plucked from a tree
and it tasted sweet on their tongues that were pink.
They saw all the butterflies with their big blue eyes
and glimpsed the hummingbirds if they didn't blink.
The wind was blowing through the trees,
so Jack had his girls close their eyes.
They used their ears to hear the sound
that made them fall asleep and dad heard their sighs.

☺ ☺

January ②⑤
(Day 25 of 366)

Let's see what the Bible📖 has to say:

✝ Proverbs 3:17 Her ways are pleasant ways, and all her paths are peace.

**D.J. knows that Jesus really walked the earth,
because in human form, God Himself made.
Then He suffered, died and rose again
for all of us – our ransom is paid!**

✝

January ❷❻

(Day 26 of 366)

Let's see what the Bible📖 has to say:

✝ 1 Timothy 2:5–6 For there is one God and one mediator between God and men, the man Christ Jesus, who gave Himself as a ransom for all men – the testimony given in its proper time.

Some people scoff at the Bible,
saying the Flood was not world-wide.
Buddy learned that many cultures
have legends to prove the other side.
If the Flood was going to be local,
Buddy is pretty sure it would be found
that instead of God telling Noah to build an ark,
He would have told him to move to higher ground.

January ②⑦
(Day 27 of 366)

Let's see what the Bible📖 has to say:

✝ 2 Peter 3:3 First of all, you must understand that in the last days scoffers will come, scoffing and following their own evil desires.

When Kimberella wrote her first book,
she almost put it away to forget.
Prince Roderick saw what was happening
and helped her just like he did when they met.
He convinced her she needed to publish it,
since she worked so hard to write it all down.
Besides, he knew she felt she was called to create...
devotionals, even though she acts like a clown.
God uses us all by giving us talents and gifts
and it would be a shame if we don't see them as such.
This is now Mrs. Buckskins' fourth attempt,
hoping that just *one* person feels God's loving touch.

January ❷❽
(Day 28 of 366)

Let's see what the Bible📖 has to say:

✝ **1** John 4:16 We are from God, and whoever knows God listens to us, but whoever is not from God does not listen to us. This is how we recognize the Spirit of truth and the spirit of falsehood.

Rochelle turned to her Bible
to learn about worship
as she was finishing up her coffee
in the breakfast booth.
The Book of John said that God is spirit
and those who worship Him
must worship in spirit
and let's not forget to worship in truth.

January ❷❾

(Day 29 of 366)

Let's see what the Bible📖 has to say:

✝ John 4:24 "God is spirit, and His worshippers must worship in spirit and in truth."

Chew-Chew wants to talk about symbiosis,
which is a big subject for such a little guy.
He's used to saying goo-goo, gaga
while chomping on a wedge of blueberry pie.
There are fish that clean other fishes' teeth
and they swim right into their mouth.
The fish the others are cleaning
has a lot of teeth on the north and the south.
Those same big fish will eat all kinds of things,
including little fishies that come swimming along.
For some strange reason, or at least to Chew-Chew,
they won't eat what's *in* their mouth like King Kong.
Could it be that God created them this way
and one gets a free lunch and the other a shiny fang?
This little tyke would rather buy *that* theory
than fall for the coincidental result of the Big Bang.

January 30

(Day 30 of 366)

Let's see what the Bible📖 has to say:

✝ Amos 4:6 "I gave you empty stomachs in every city
and lack of bread in every town, yet you have not returned
to me," declares the Lord.

**Rain, snow and beautiful sunshine
were all created for our benefit.
Without them we would be lost
like Fudgy without his dim wit.**

January ❸❶
(Day 31 of 366)

Let's see what the Bible has to say:

† Colossians 4:6 Let your conversation be always full of grace, seasoned with salt, so that you may know how to answer everyone.

Chew-Chew asked his father,
"Can I go out and play?"
The General told him he'll have to wait
to hear what the weatherman has to say.
He flipped on the radio
and muted the T.V.,
so he could listen to one
and with the other, take a look-see.
"Global Warming" is causing the heat,
"Climate Change" is for when it's *not* hot.
Chew-Chew just wants to go outside,
but The General will tell him when *to* or to *not*.
He heard that we broke a record from back when,
about one hundred and fifty years ago.
He wondered if that means we were under a threat
when the sun in February melted the snow.
Chew-Chew's dad dressed him up
with a hat, sunglasses and for each foot, a boot.
He wanted to cover all of his bases –
Jules took a picture, since he was SO cute!

February ❶
(Day 32 of 366)

Let's see what the Bible📖 has to say:

† Genesis 8:22 "As long as the earth endures, seed time and harvest, cold and heat, summer and winter, day and night will never cease."

**Witty Kitty knows that God designed his body
with all different parts to make him fully functioning.
He can climb trees, jump to a high shelf,
and put his ears back while listening to Fudgy sing.
God, who is smarter than we will *ever* know,
knew to use the eyeball, joints, and
muscles, to name a few
on *all* of His Creation, proving an intelligent Designer,
not that we all came from the same patch of slimy goo.**

🐈

February ❷

(Day 33 of 366)

Let's see what the Bible📖 has to say:

[†] 2 Timothy 4:4 They will turn their ears away from the truth and turn aside to myths.

Mary Lu put on her sunglasses
as she played upon a sandy beach.
The sun was ever so very bright,
that it was almost within her reach.
She heard once that earth was billions of years old
and also that the sun is shrinking in size.
Mary Lu thought as she built her castle,
"If this is true, than no need of these for eyes."

February ❸

(Day 34 of 366)

Let's see what the Bible📖 has to say:

✝ Matthew 5:45 "That you may be sons of your Father in Heaven. He causes the sun to rise on the evil and good, and sends rain on the righteous and the unrighteous."

Sometimes people think they are so intelligent –
almost as if they are too smart for God.
Kimberella would like to see a human being
not only make a fish, but be specific and make a cod.

February ❹
(Day 35 of 366)

Let's see what the Bible📖 has to say:

✝ Matthew 13:47 "Once again, the Kingdom of Heaven is like a net that was let down into the lake and caught all kinds of fish."

The General took a field trip with his son's class
and sat in a prairie that consisted of mostly grass.
The ranger gave them each a pair of binoculars
to be able to see through the weeds' sticky burrs.
"You can see the birds use their wings to fly over you,"
Chew-Chew knew *that* much and he's only two.
"Why do some birds have wings, but cannot fly?"
the lad asked the ranger as he walked on by.
"So they can signal to the others from the ground."
The General rolled his eyes and didn't utter a sound.
God designed birds with wings, made with a feather
that can make them fly in all kinds of weather.
If you find one on the ground, walking down a path,
put it in your hat or a vase that you keep by your bath.

February ❺
(Day 36 of 366)

Let's see what the Bible📖 has to say:

✝ Isaiah 40:31 But those who hope in the Lord will renew their strength.

**Today when Jack read his Bible,
it talked about respect.
As someone who looks up to his elders,
he liked this subject very much.
Whenever he sees someone heading
towards an entrance to a store,
he runs to hold the door open,
especially if they are using a crutch.**

February ❻

(Day 37 of 366)

Let's see what the Bible📖 has to say:

† Leviticus 19:32 'Rise in the presence of the aged, show respect for the elderly and revere your God. I am the Lord.'

Witty Kitty wants to know if you are saved?
If so, were you also baptized?
Jesus was baptized, but not as a baby, then He suffered,
died, was buried and rose to be at His Father's side.
By repentance of our sins, our old selves die,
by submersion in water in Jesus' name, we are buried.
We receive the Holy Spirit, which resurrected Jesus.
***We* become the Church when Christ gets married.**

≋≋≋≋≋≋≋

February ❼
(Day 38 of 366)

Let's see what the Bible has to say:

✝ Revelation 19:7 Let us rejoice and be glad and give Him glory! For the wedding of the Lamb has come, and His bride has made herself ready.

If the universe started "In the beginning",
like Prince Roderick knows the Bible has written,
then you can count back the generations...
to figure out years – use a glove instead of a mitten.

February ❽
(Day 39 of 366)

Let's see what the Bible📖 has to say:

✝ Genesis 1:1 In the beginning God created the heavens and the earth.

D.J. likes the taste of barbequed chicken
that was cooked on a smoking hot grill.
He also likes a side order of French fries,
especially if someone else is flipping the bill.
The band member will follow it up every time
with a banana shake and extra whipped cream.
If a cherry was placed on top of the dessert,
he would think he's in a fantastic dream.
Why all of this talk about D.J.'s tastes in food,
wasting everyone who's reading this time?
Because without taste buds to enjoy our food,
it would be like listening to a story from a mime.

February ❾
(Day 40 of 366)

Let's see what the Bible📖 has to say:

† Ecclesiastes 5:12 The sleep of a laborer is sweet, whether he eats little or much, but the abundance of a rich man permits him no sleep.

Jules prefers to believe in Almighty God,
who had a purpose to design His Creation.
She knows her belief is called religion,
but she *also* knows that so is Evolution.

†

February ❶⓪

(Day 41 of 366)

Let's see what the Bible has to say:

⊺ James 1:27 Religion that God our Father accepts as pure and faultless is this: to look after orphans and widows in their distress and to keep oneself from being polluted by the world.

If Kimberella were aboard Noah's ark,
she would have studied the sloth.
It wouldn't be much of a study though,
since she flitters around like a moth.
The moth is related to butterflies,
but instead of the day, they prefer the night.
Butterflies have clubs at the end of their antennas
and moths just bang their heads against a light.

≈≈≈◇≈≈≈

February ❶❶
(Day 42 of 366)

Let's see what the Bible📖 has to say:

† Luke 12:33 Sell your possessions and give to the poor. Provide purses for yourselves that will not wear out, a treasure in Heaven that will not be exhausted, where no thief comes near and no moth destroys.

**Fudgy says if you need proof of the great Flood,
you do not have to travel very far.
Just head west to South Dakota
and you'll find some shark teeth in a jar.**

VVVVV
ΛΛΛΛΛ

February ❶❷
(Day 43 of 366)

Let's see what the Bible has to say:

☦ Isaiah 6:8 Then I heard the voice of the Lord saying, "When shall I send? And who will go for us?" And I said, "Here am I. Send me!"

Rochelle tries to set a good example
as a Christian wherever she may be.
If she's in a grocery store waiting in line
or playing alongside strangers in the sea.
Actions speaks louder than words,
or at least that's what is preached.
She knows that if she doesn't watch it,
the idea of being a Christian could be breached.

February ❶❸
(Day 44 of 366)

Let's see what the Bible📖 has to say:

† Matthew 15:11 What goes into a man's mouth does not make him 'unclean', but what comes out of his mouth, that is what makes him 'unclean'.

Lucifer was called the Angel of Light
when he resided in Heaven above.
When he fell, he took a third of the angels with him.
Prince Roderick says they rejected God's love.
Are you rejecting God's love
while residing here on earth?
Please choose to be with God eternally,
since He's the one who knew you before birth.

♥ ✎ ✝

February ❶❹
(Day 45 of 366)

Let's see what the Bible📖 has to say:

✝ Matthew 25:41 "Then He will say to those on His left, 'Depart from me, you who are cursed, into the eternal fire prepared for the devil and his angels.'"

**When Buddy reads "billions of years"
given for the universe's age,
he just skips over that part
as he sips his coffee and turns the page.**

February ❶❺

(Day 46 of 366)

Let's see what the Bible has to say:

✝ Matthew 22:5 "But they paid no attention and went off – one to his field, another to his business."

The General was on his driveway
late one wintery night.
When he looked up to the sky above
and saw a spectacular sight.
A comet was whizzing across the great expanse
and he told his daughter and his son,
"A comet is made from ice and dust –
the tail is from gas that will shine until it's done."

☾ ★ ★ ★

February ❶❻

(Day 47 of 366)

Let's see what the Bible has to say:

† Job 37:10 The breath of God produces ice, and the broad water become frozen.

**Jack wants to ask you a question about Evolution:
"What's the difference between macro and micro?"
Macro needs magic involving billions of years,
but micro is a little change, like thicker hair on a doe.**

< vs. >

February ❶❼

(Day 48 of 366)

Let's see what the Bible📖 has to say:

✝ James 1:5 If any of you lacks wisdom, he should ask God, who gives generously to all without finding fault, and it will be given to him.

When you find yourself fighting against a giant
that creeps up during your life once in a while,
D.J. says to ask God in Jesus' name to fight for you,
but you will still need to rise up and jump on the pile.

February ❶❽

(Day 49 of 366)

Let's see what the Bible📖 has to say:

✝ **P**salm 24:8 Who is this King of glory? The Lord strong
and mighty, the Lord mighty in battle.

Kimberella laughs when she listens to talk of Evolution
trying to explain the reproductive system's plight.
Because a male and female (you choose the species)
would keep starting over and over to get it right.
Even if in your wildest dreams one of them *does* succeed,
he or she would have to wait for the other to do the same
and then would die and have to start over again.
How many millions of years would be this game?
That's just *one* species, which would
be a miracle for sure.
Then you would hope that a baby is the final result.
All the species in the world would
go through this process?
Please know God designed it and
Evolution is a major insult!

February ❶❾
(Day 50 of 366)

Let's see what the Bible📖 has to say:

✝ Psalm 139:13 For you created my inmost being; you
knit me together in my mother's womb.

Today when Chew-Chew read his Bible,
it talked about truth.
He didn't really read it,
but his mommy filled him in with couth:
"Little children should not love
just in word or in talk.....
but in deed and in truth –
now go take a walk."

February ❷⓿
(Day 51 of 366)

Let's see what the Bible📖 has to say:

✝ 1 John 3:18 Dear children, let us not love with words or tongue but with actions and in truth.

Izzy Ann can see things clearly –
she perceives depth, looking at width and height.
It's what you call the three dimensions,
like a graham cracker before the first bite.
What if God uses *four* dimensions
or even more than *that*?
It's too much for our brains to handle,
like when He created the body to fit under a hat.

February ➋➊

(Day 52 of 366)

Let's see what the Bible📖 has to say:

✝ Genesis 6:15 This is how you are to build it: The ark is to be 450 feet long, 75 feet wide and 45 feet high.

Prince Roderick had to take Fudgy to the Veterinarian.
He opened up the closet and grabbed
the pooch's muzzle.
After a thorough examination and a couple of x-rays,
the vet discovered that he swallowed a piece of puzzle.
Mr. Buckskin was in awe, seeing
the bones in the picture.
He knew there would be quite a few larger ones,
but he just couldn't believe what he saw –
the skull was much smaller, like
the size of cocktail buns.
He figured Fudgy would have a much larger skull,
since his head looked so huge with all his fur.
It did kind of make sense to the prince, however,
because he acts like a baby, as it were.
He told Kimberella when he arrived back home,
holding the missing puzzle piece in his hand,
"God for sure used the same design with bones
for all kinds of animals throughout the land."

February ❷❷

(Day 53 of 366)

Let's see what the Bible📖 has to say:

✝ Psalm 34:20 He protects all his bones, not one of them
will be broken.

Sara-Sara told her class one day
that the moon is what causes the tide.
God planned on making it that way
at this, the children opened their eyes up wide.
He added some salt to the sea
and the creatures in it were pleased,
because if black pepper was added instead,
they couldn't swim and would have sneezed.

ACHOO!

February ❷❸

(Day 54 of 366)

Let's see what the Bible📖 has to say:

✝ Matthew 5:13 "You are the salt of the earth. But if the salt loses its saltiness, how can it be made salty again? It is no longer good for anything, except to be thrown out and trampled by men."

Buddy went to work, but the doors were boarded shut.
A sign posted said: "Sorry, but we had to close up shop."
Circumstances can change, like
making an animal balloon
and it builds character each time *your* balloon will pop.

"BUSINESS CLOSED"

February ❷❹
(Day 55 of 366)

Let's see what the Bible📖 has to say:

† Luke 1:37 "For nothing is impossible with God."

"When did time start?" Fudgy asked Witty Kitty.
"Genesis 1:1 says, 'In the beginning'", and so it went.
Witty Kitty added, "Time just started for us to use,
because God lives in the past, future and present.
He sees everything all at one time,
where we can only be in one place.
God can see you as a little puppy,
but I can only see your now-a-day face."

February ❷❺

(Day 56 of 366)

Let's see what the Bible📖 has to say:

† Genesis 1:1 In the beginning God created the Heaven and the earth.

You can look at the Book of Revelation
as a kind of prediction of sorts.
D.J. says that God already knows the ending
regarding Satan and his evil cohorts.
We all have free will and go about our day,
whether we choose to follow Jesus is up to us.
So instead of it being a prediction,
it's how it played out and is too late to fuss.
The tribulation *will* happen as the Bible is written.
If you want to be on the road to Heaven that is paved,
please ask Jesus to forgive your sins
and your belief in Him will get you saved!

✝

February ②⑥

(Day 57 of 366)

Let's see what the Bible📖 has to say:

† Joshua 24:15 "But if serving the Lord seems undesirable to you, then choose for yourselves this day whom you will serve, whether the gods your forefathers served beyond the River, or the gods of the Amorites, in whose land you are living. But as for me and my household, we will serve the Lord."

**The General turned to his Bible to learn how to fast
as he was thinking about days gone past.
The Book of Psalms says to become humbled
through weeping and fasting to see how you fumbled.**

February ❷❼
(Day 58 of 366)

Let's see what the Bible📖 has to say:

[†] Psalm 69:10 When I weep and fast, I must endure scorn;

Fudgy is just a dog with a human brain,
but he is fictional, not a fluke of Evolution.
If he were real and could *really* read,
he would say, "It's true from start 'til done."
It's better and just makes sense
to believe that the Bible is true,
than not to believe God's Word
and later having the truth make you blue.
If the Bible is true, Fudgy has it made;
if the Bible is not true, he'll just be dead.
If the unbeliever is right, he'll just be dust;
if He's wrong, he'll see lots of red.
Please don't wait until it's too late
and stop making excuses to not believe.
Start having faith in God and His Word.
It's okay to wear your heart on your sleeve.

February ➋➑

(Day 59 of 366)

Let's see what the Bible📖 has to say:

† Psalm 14:1 The fool says in his heart, "There is no God."
They are corrupt, their deeds are vile; there is no one who
does good.

**Auntie K.T. has some good advice
about drinking tea with ginseng.
It's great for your mind, the internet says,
but not if your mind can't handle the zing!**

≳ 😐 ≲

February ❷❾

(Day 60 of 366)

Let's see what the Bible📖 has to say:

✝ 3 John 1:2 Dear friend, I pray that you may enjoy good health and that all may go well with you, even as your soul is getting along well.

Jules' favorite animal is a cow.....moo!
In fact, she has liked them since the age of two.
She heard it said that they release methane gas
while eating in the pasture during their daily pass.
Scientists say that it's causing harm to the ozone,
so she ran over to use her parents' phone.
"Hello? Do you think we are all *that* dumb?
If it *is* true, please try feeding them a Tum!"

March ❶

(Day 61 of 366)

Let's see what the Bible📖 has to say:

✝ 1 Samuel 6:7 "Now then, get a new cart ready, with two cows that have calved and have never been yoked. Hitch the cows to the cart, but take their calves away and pen them up."

Izzy Ann has been told that she is smart,
which brings much happiness and joy to her heart.
In Sunday School she learned about getting wisdom –
just figure out what God wants and it will come.

♥

March ❷
(Day 62 of 366)

Let's see what the Bible has to say:

† Proverbs 18:15 The heart of the discerning acquires knowledge; the ears of the wise seek it out.

The eyeball is an amazing thing
designed to see all of God's Creation.
It's made up of many components
and all are needed throughout our duration.
Prince Roderick asks, "If we evolved,
then how many tries did it take
to get everything just right
after crawling out of the lake?
Did we form one part of the eye
and live out our years half-blind?
Then someone else had to try to evolve,
magically causing the mystery to unwind?"
Think of all the living creatures,
that have an eye as part of their being:
bugs, animals, birds and fishes
to be "lucky" enough to make an eye for their seeing.
Mr. Buckskin believes that God did the designing
of the eyes, ears and the rest of our face,
so we can see and hear what God's Word teaches
about *His* Creation on a case-by-case.

👁 👁 ◉ ◉

March ❸

(Day 63 of 366)

Let's see what the Bible has to say:

✝ Proverbs 20:12 Ears that hear and eyes that see – the Lord has made them both.

Which came first – the chicken or the egg?
Chew-Chew says the chicken did, of course.
The Bible says that God made all of the animals,
which included eggs inside their original source.
He asked his mommy if they can have some birds
to keep penned up in the back yard.
He added that they can collect eggs every morning.
Jules said, "How many?" "3 and make the yolks hard."

March ❹

(Day 64 of 366)

Let's see what the Bible📖 has to say:

✝ Luke 11:12 Or if he asks for an egg, will you give him a scorpion?

When D.J. is working hard at his job
and a co-worker warns, "Stop! And you better had!"
He will ask them, "Why?" and they will say,
"Because so-and-so might get mad."
"Who is this so-and-so who might get mad?
Is he or she my superior?"
"No, just another person on your line
that doesn't want you to make *them* look inferior."
"My intention is to do my job the way I said I would
when I was being interviewed by my boss.
I can't help it if they strayed so far away,
that their duties include applying lip gloss!"
We tend to take our work for granted,
which seems to be a trend right now.
We should act like it's our very first day
and work as a team and not have a cow.
Think back to when you were answering questions
and you said that you would follow the rules.
You didn't say that you need time for things like
sleeping, texting and using manicuring tools.
D.J. gets tired of hearing that someone might get mad
to stop him from doing what he was hired to do.
He'd like to say, "Build a bridge and get over it!",
but he's afraid *that* statement *would* start a coo.

March ❺

(Day 65 of 366)

Let's see what the Bible📖 has to say:

✝ Psalm 37:8 Refrain from anger and turn from wrath; do not fret – it leads only to evil.

God made a variety of food for us to enjoy,
therefore, Buddy thinks that God must really care.
There's beef, pork, foul and fish,
squirrel, rabbit, deer and bear.
If the latter just upset your stomach
and you think Buddy's brain stopped tickin',
it may help you to understand him better
that to *him*, *all* meat tastes just like chicken.

March ❻

(Day 66 of 366)

Let's see what the Bible📖 has to say:

✝ **1** Corinthians 15:39 All flesh is not the same: men have one kind of flesh, animals have another, birds another and fish another.

God must have a sense of humor
and a soft spot for the cuteness of a kitten.
Why else would He create the babies
of animals and humans for us to be smitten?
Does He look upon all of His Creation
of living things no matter how old they are...
and say to His angels around Him,
"Oh, look at the cute baby driving his car!"

March ❼
(Day 67 of 366)

Let's see what the Bible has to say:

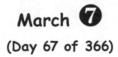 Isaiah 53:4 Surely He took up our infirmities and carried our sorrows, yet we considered Him stricken by God, smitten by Him, and afflicted.

Kimberella turned to her Bible
to learn how to prepare bread,
because somehow, she didn't believe
in what Prince Roderick had said.
The Book of Ezekiel said to take wheat,
barley, beans and lentil,
then toss in millet and emmer
and to use a single vessel.

March ❽

(Day 68 of 366)

Let's see what the Bible📖 has to say:

✝ **Ezekiel 4:9** "Take wheat and barley, beans and lentils, millet and spelt; put them in a storage jar and use them to make bread for yourself. You are to eat it during the 390 days you lie on your side."

Izzy Ann wanted to have a rocket ship built
for her to go visit the moon.
She saw his face in a dream
and thought that she better go soon.
She heard that the universe is billions of years old
and the earth's moon is receding.
If that's correct, the earth and moon would have been
closer than a bottle and a baby at feeding.

March ❾

(Day 69 of 366)

Let's see what the Bible📖 has to say:

✝ **Psalm** 89:37 " 'It will be established forever like the moon, the faithful witness in the sky'."

**Sara-Sara turned on the telly
to get the weather report.
She heard that it's going to be hot,
so to drink water by the quart.
"Don't worry," her husband scolded,
"it's a dry heat, so it won't sicken."
"Oh great, so my skin will be like beef jerky,
rather than a juicy rotisserie chicken!"**

March ❶⓪

(Day 70 of 366)

Let's see what the Bible has to say:

† Genesis 8:22 "As long as the earth endures, seedtime and harvest, cold and heat, summer and winter, day and night will never cease."

Auntie K.T. went to her cupboard
to find herself an old mug.
She likes to use it in her yard
while searching for that perfect bug.
She wades through the grass
that's supposed to be long
and then swings through the trees –
kind of like (but not quite) King Kong.
K.T. needs a lid for her cup,
because it's a jungle out there.
Something like 5,000 different grasses
and 100,000 plants, so our earth isn't bare.

March ❶❶

(Day 71 of 366)

Let's see what the Bible📖 has to say:

✝ Isaiah 40:8 "The grass withers and the flowers fall, but the Word of our God stands forever."

**If Jack were aboard Noah's ark,
he would have studied the mole,
which comes to mind...did they have dirt for him,
so he could dig while playing his role?
The mole has a cylinder body
and his fur is soft and velvety.
He has very small ears and eyes
to keep from getting totally dirty.**

≈≈≈◇≈≈≈

March ❶❷

(Day 72 of 366)

Let's see what the Bible📖 has to say:

✝ **Genesis 3:19** "By the sweat of your brow you will eat your food until you return to the ground, since from it you were taken; for dust you are and to dust you will return."

**Witty Kitty went to Loch Ness
to look up an old time friend.
When Nessie appeared, he put back his ears,
'cause she passed him and swam around the bend!**

≈≈≈≈≈≈≈≈≈≈

March ❶❸

(Day 73 of 366)

Let's see what the Bible📖 has to say:

† Psalm 8:8 The birds of the air, and the fish of the sea, all that swim the paths of the seas.

**Since Sara-Sara teaches children all day,
she knows how important discipline can be.
When they took God out of the classroom,
the problems with students became easy to see.
Not just in school, the lack of faith can be at home.
Kids act like animals, so the teachers' hands are tied.
Please teach your kids about God and Creation,
because books push Evolution and not the other side.**

March ❶❹

(Day 74 of 366)

Let's see what the Bible📖 has to say:

† Romans 1:21 For although they knew God, they neither glorified Him as God nor gave thanks to Him, but their thinking became futile and their foolish hearts were darkened.

Can worrying be a sin?
Maybe not, if you just visit.
Jack says not to stay *too* long
and to trust in Jesus to get over it.

March ❶❺

(Day 75 of 366)

Let's see what the Bible📖 has to say:

✝ Philippians 4:6 Do not be anxious about anything, but in everything, by prayer and petition with thanksgiving, present your request to God.

People who believe in the theory of Evolution,
believe that things get better with time.
Let's look at the aging process,
which *could* be considered a crime.
A baby needs help eating her meals,
taking a bath and getting dressed.
A hundred year old needs the same assistance,
so far, Prince Roderick is *not* impressed.
A grade school child learns how to read,
loves her recess and learns to do math.
An elderly person can't see the fine print,
counts her fingers, which arthritis raged its wrath.
A teenager wants to learn how to drive
and takes the appropriate test.
Prince Roderick knows the *real* trial is
telling Grandma *not* driving would be the best.
You put a magnet on your fridge
with a saying written by a sage:
*"Forty is the old age of youth
and fifty is the youth of old age."*
You can *believe* whatever you *want* to believe,
but as for Mr. Buckskin, he knows what is true –
Nothing gets better and stronger with time
and *God* created it all, so let's give Him *His* due!

March ❶❻

(Day 76 of 366)

Let's see what the Bible📖 has to say:

✝ Ecclesiastes 12:1 Remember your Creator in the days
of your youth, before the days of trouble come and the years
approach when you will say, "I find no pleasure in them."

Mary Lu watched the Ten Commandments
with her Grandma and Grandpa Buckskin.
It came to the part where people worshipped the idol
and she used her hands to prop up her chin.
"Isn't that the wrong thing for them to do?"
Grandpa replied, "Of course, look at Moses' face!"
She watched him throw the tablets to the ground,
because what they were doing was a total disgrace.

March ❶❼
(Day 77 of 366)

Let's see what the Bible📖 has to say:

✝ Leviticus 19:4 "'Do not turn to idols or make gods of cast metal for yourselves. I am the Lord your God.'"

Rochelle took a correspondence course on-line
to study science at home for fun at her leisure.
If she told you that someone created life in a lab,
it would be amazing and you would also concur.
If creating a single cell is absolutely exciting
and it took loads of intelligence to make it happen,
then think how amazing God must be
to create it all, for example: the egg *and* the hen.
Rochelle wrote an essay on the subject at hand,
that intelligence is needed for such a feat.
The theory of Evolution is just a fairy tale
and she sent it to her teacher without missing a beat.

March ❶❽

(Day 78 of 366)

Let's see what the Bible📖 has to say:

✝ Hebrews 3:4 For every house is built by someone, but God is the builder of everything.

At Vacation Bible School one summer,
Izzy Ann learned the books of the Bible in order.
That's pretty impressive for a four year old,
even if her fifth birthday is right on the border.
"The Book of Revelation is at the very end,"
she reported to her mother, Jules,
"and everyone should read it today
to learn what happens if you break God's rules."
Genesis, Exodus......Revelation

March ❶❾

(Day 79 of 366)

Let's see what the Bible has to say:

✝ Revelation 1:1 The revelation of Jesus Christ, which God gave Him to show His servants what must soon take place. He made it known by sending His angel to His servant John.

One very hot summer day,
Mrs. Buckskin painted Nessie on her driveway.
Snakes thought it was their king
and swarmed around it in a ring.
She could see that they were a bunch of babies,
but she foamed at the mouth like she had rabies.
She hoisted the yard art into her garden
and begged the serpents for their pardon.
Kimberella says lifting 300 pounds of concrete
could be classified as quite a feat,
but when six pairs of snake eyes are upon you,
a princess gotta do what a princess gotta do!

⊙⊙　⊙⊙　⊙⊙
⊙⊙　⊙⊙　⊙⊙

March 2️0️
(Day 80 of 366)

Let's see what the Bible📖 has to say:

✝ Micah 7:17 They will lick dust like a snake, like creatures that crawl on the ground. They will come trembling out of their dens; they will turn in fear to the Lord our God and will be afraid of you.

Rock layers – schmock layers...
now Sara-Sara won't go *that* far,
because she knows that everyone
can see them while riding in their car.
There was a world-wide Flood, you see,
that cut through soft sediment.
Instead of billions of year to form,
it was quick – the waters were Heaven-sent.

March ❷❶
(Day 81 of 366)

Let's see what the Bible📖 has to say:

✝ Psalm 104:8 They flowed over the mountains, they went down into the valleys, to the place you assigned for them.

**Prince Roderick doesn't buy the Evolution theory,
but sometimes he tries to picture
a male and a female forming themselves,
then having to evolve the drive and the lure.
This all, of course, would have to happen
at the very same time as the other,
otherwise you would have a mother without a father
or a wannabe father without a mother.**

March ❷❷
(Day 82 of 366)

Let's see what the Bible📖 has to say:

✝ **Proverbs 18:22 He who finds a wife finds what is good and receives favor from the Lord.**

Today when Baby No-No read her Bible,
it talked about sin.
Since she is only an infant,
she had her daddy read the words.
When she gets older
and makes choices on her own,
she'll find out to change her ways,
because sinning is for the birds!

March ❷❸

(Day 83 of 366)

Let's see what the Bible has to say:

Proverbs 18:3 When wickedness comes, so does contempt, and with shame comes disgrace.

If the Flood of the Bible was just a local thing,
then can you please explain this to D.J. –
Why were there oodles of petrified clams
found on Mount Everest during a field day?
Is it because the Flood happened across the earth
and things were buried and such?
The mountains arose and the valleys sank down,
so clams on a mountain wouldn't take that much.

≈≈≈≈≈≈
ΛΛΛΛΛΛ

March ➋➍

(Day 84 of 366)

Let's see what the Bible has to say:

† Psalm 104:6 You covered it with the deep as with a garment; the waters stood above the mountains.

Auntie K.T., who lives out of state,
has been in a tizzy as of late.
She has a banana tree growing in her yard
and picking the fruit is just a tad bit hard.
She said to her cool neighbor, Mr. Frost,
"If a man made this tree, think of the cost!
Scientists by the scores, plus a dozen
would be gathered around with minds a buzzin'.
First a type of wood would have to be chosen
and the location, so the fruit won't get frozen.
Then instead of it growing a leaf, grow a palm.
Now to design the fruit and try to remain calm.
What texture? What size? What nutrients or shape?
It will also need a type of covering, possibly a cape.
Let's start off with a seed and plant it in the ground,
add water, sunshine and mulch in a mound.
If they can pack all those ideas into one little seed,
give them all a cigar for a job well done...indeed!"

March ❷❺

(Day 85 of 366)

Let's see what the Bible📖 has to say:

✝ Isaiah 29:14 "Therefore once more I will astound these people with wonder upon wonder; the wisdom of the wise will perish, the intelligence of the intelligent will vanish."

Lanore just turned three, which is quite a big to-do
and if she lives to be a hundred, it would be astounding.
Think of the presents she would
open during her lifetime,
the number they would represent would be abounding.
The little tyke learned in Sunday School last week
that some people, before the Flood, lived to be really old.
Her grandpa added that it might be from an ice ring
slowing down their aging or possibly being put on hold.
After the rain came down from the ring above,
their protection disappeared just like that.
Now humans are lucky to make it to be one hundred,
even with sunscreen, long sleeves
and a wide-rimmed hat.

👓 *100* 👓

March ❷❻
(Day 86 of 366)

Let's see what the Bible📖 has to say:

† Genesis 5:27 Altogether, Methuselah lived 969 years, and then he died.

**Baby No-No was told not to touch Mr. Sasquatch
if the two of them met face to face.
Being a baby who is strong-willed, at best,
said, "His hair felt like a hippy's suitcase!"**

March ❷❼
(Day 87 of 366)

Let's see what the Bible📖 has to say:

✝ Judges 13:5 "Because you will conceive and give birth to a son. No razor may be used on his head, because the boy is to be a Nazirite, set apart to God from birth, and he will begin the deliverance of Israel from the hands of the Philistines."

The General likes to hear straight answers –
this is a statement you can be sure.
So when someone explains with circular reasoning,
it's like placing under his saddle, a burr.
He took in a sample of a fossil to have the thing dated
and was told that the fossil was as old as the rock.
He then asked them how old the rock layers were
and they asked for his fossil back that was in his sock.

↺   ↻

March ❷❽
(Day 88 of 366)

Let's see what the Bible📖 has to say:

✝ Psalm 90:10 The length of our days is seventy years – or eighty, if we have the strength; yet their span is but trouble and sorrow, for they quickly pass, and we fly away.

Rochelle was reading her Bible
and came to the Book of Revelation.
The mark of the beast was mentioned,
which made her want to run.
The number is six hundred sixty-six
and the mark will be used to buy and sell.
Whatever you do, *do not* accept the mark,
so you will spend eternity in Heaven and not in Hell!

666

March ❷❾

(Day 89 of 366)

Let's see what the Bible📖 has to say:

✝ Revelation 13:17 So that no one could buy or sell unless he had the mark, which is the name of the beast or the number of his name.

Kimberella doesn't understand how a person can believe
in the Big Gap theory, allowing years of time in between.
On Day number four, God created the vegetation
and the next Day He created the
sun to help keep it green.
If you put a thousand years in between the two days,
like some interpreters would like to think conspired,
then Mrs. Buckskin would venture a guess
the crisp celery she's used to would
look pretty much tired.
Let's face it, the Big Gap theory
just went down the tubes,
faster than water going down a freshly cleaned drain.
If you don't want to believe this is true,
try eating watermelon grown in a desert with no rain.

🏝 + *1,000 years* ✸ = 🏜

March 3⓪

(Day 90 of 366)

Let's see what the Bible📖 has to say:

† Exodus 20:11 For in six days the Lord made the heavens
and the earth, the sea, and all that is in them, but He rested
on the seventh day. Therefore the Lord blessed the Sabbath
day and made it holy.

Buddy turned to his Bible
to learn how to fish.
When he blew out his birthday candles,
this was his wish.
The Book of Matthew said to use
a net and plenty you will find.
Like in the Kingdom of Heaven,
gathering fish of every kind.

March ❸❶
(Day 91 of 366)

Let's see what the Bible📖 has to say:

✝ Matthew 13:47 "Once again, the Kingdom of Heaven is like a net that was let down into the lake and caught all kinds of fish."

The General decided to use some donuts
to try to catch a Sasquatch.
He saw it on T.V. one night
and set the trap along with his watch.
He also sprinkled some magic powder
to help track any footprints.
In the morning what he saw
was a mound of peanuts and some pillow mints.
It appeared that Kimberella
spent the night up in a tree.
Seeing the powder, she used a rope
and took not one donut, but three.
She didn't leave a footprint
or even a trace of hair,
but The General knew who did it,
along with the why, what *and* where.
Prince Roderick came down the trail
and hollered with all of his might,
"Big Foot must wear shoes...
come take a look at this sight!"
He saw his son-in-law guiding
his pretty Doll by the elbow
to the pickup truck for punishment
as she chomped on a marshmallow.
The General then told Mr. Buckskin,
"Those are *my* prints, not *his*."
His father-in-law lost his pep
like a mug of root beer without its fizz.

● ● ●

April ❶

(Day 92 of 366)

Let's see what the Bible📖 has to say:

✝ Matthew 3:10 The ax is already at the root of the trees; and every tree that does not produce good fruit will be cut down and thrown into the fire.

**Chew-Chew can catch a ball
if you throw it carefully towards his way.
His reflexes were designed very carefully
to save you a trip to the doctor today.**

April ❷
(Day 93 of 366)

Let's see what the Bible📖 has to say:

✝ Philippians 4:13 I can do everything through Him who gives me strength.

Jules told her mother that you shrink during the day and have to adjust the rearview mirror driving home. Kimberella said, "I use it to apply my lipstick and such and *then* to see how much gray hair I have to comb."

April ❸

(Day 94 of 366)

Let's see what the Bible📖 has to say:

✝ 1 Samuel 16:7 But the Lord said to Samuel, "Do not consider his appearance or his height, for I have rejected him. The Lord does not look at the things man looks at. Man looks at the outward appearance, but the Lord looks at the heart."

To be smart is a wonderful thing.
The opposite of highs is lows,
two plus twelve is fourteen –
and so the testing goes.
But Witty Kitty thinks it's smart to be wise
and figure out what God *really* meant
when He talked about *kinds* of animals
who boarded the ark free of rent.
He *didn't* say to Noah,
"Load up the cheetahs, cougars and panthers."
He just said to take two of the cat kind,
otherwise, there would be *way* too many furs.

April ❹

(Day 95 of 366)

Let's see what the Bible📖 has to say:

⊤ Genesis 6:20 Two of every kind of bird, of every kind of animal and of every kind of creature that moves along the ground will come to you to be kept alive.

Mary Lu learned at Bible Camp
that if you don't work, you don't eat.
That can make even an eight year old
be mindful and think on her feet.
The Bible says just that,
however, just so you know...
the exceptions are the sick and elderly,
and also a child or a lonely widow.

April ❺

(Day 96 of 366)

Let's see what the Bible📖 has to say:

† **2 Thessalonians 3:10** For even when we were with you, we gave you this rule: "If a man will not work, he shall not eat."

Imagine a tornado running through a junk yard
and given billions of years to do it.
Also imagine that all the parts needed are in the pile
to assemble a jet, down to every last bit.
Buddy knows that the chances would still be zero
of *ever* assembling anything close to a plane,
because chaos isn't the way things are designed
and to believe it *could* be considered insane.

April ❻
(Day 97 of 366)

Let's see what the Bible📖 has to say:

† 2 Kings 2:11 As they were walking along and talking together, suddenly a chariot of fire and horses of fire appeared and separated the two of them, and Elijah went up to heaven in a whirlwind.

Prince Roderick is an interesting man.
He's a wolf dressed up like a young king.
A caveman isn't much different, you see,
because he's a bully dressed in sheep's clothing.

☹☺   ☹☺

April ❼
(Day 98 of 366)

Let's see what the Bible has to say:

 Matthew 7:15 "Watch out for false prophets. They come to you in sheep's clothing, but inwardly they are ferocious wolves."

Jules is reluctant to talk about the nervous system,
since too many things are needed.
It takes a lot of cooperation
for the brain to have yourself seated.
All the wiring has to be just right
to send the signal from a thought
to the bottom portion of your body
to know where *not* to sit and where you *ought*.
Then you have to lower your body to the chair
and bend your knees just so
as you balance a cup of tea while humming
and watch it so you don't spill any on your toe.
You may also at the same time
be nodding at what someone just said,
while in the other hand you are holding an apple
and can identify it as being the color red.
A message at the same time is sent to your brain
that your watch say it's Two O'clock
and hoping that your child coming home from school
remembers which white house is theirs on the block.
It takes nerve to think we did this on our own –
that we were smart enough to come up with a system.
Doing this many things all at one time
takes a Designer, not something equal to a whim.

✝

April ❽

(Day 99 of 366)

Let's see what the Bible📖 has to say:

📖 Deuteronomy 6:7 Impress them on your children. Talk
about them when you sit at home and when you walk along
the road, when you lie down and when you get up.

Fudgy thinks it's cool that God knows
the number of hairs on his head.
That's a pretty good trick, since he is an
Old English sheepdog who is kept well-fed.
He has *so* much fur
that the extra hangs over his eyes.
When he stands up,
his stomach hangs over his thighs.
He thinks that the fur on his beautiful body
must be over the top.
God just counts *his* eyelashes,
since his fur is matted like an overused mop.

April ❾

(Day 100 of 366)

Let's see what the Bible📖 has to say:

✝ Matthew 10:30 And even the very hairs on your head
are all numbered.

Jack's neighbor was mowing grass at Six O'clock a.m.,
which woke him up just in time to throw a hissy fit.
He opened the window and gave a tremendous shout,
"Look, Mister...I have one nerve left and you're on it!"
We're supposed to love our neighbors, all during the day
and certain things can be the cause of the yelling wars.
It could just be that Mister Twister's Mrs.
was sick for days and he's stuck doing *all* of *her* chores.

April ①⓪
(Day 101 of 366)

Let's see what the Bible📖 has to say:

✝ Romans 13:10 Love does no harm to its neighbor. Therefore love is the fulfillment of the law.

Izzy Ann learned in Sunday School
that she should help out others.
This would include people she doesn't know
as well as any sisters or brothers.
Performing good works and deeds
are very nice gestures for sure,
but just know that's not what gets you to Heaven...
it's about what *Jesus* did and not what *you* were.

April ❶❶

(Day 102 of 366)

Let's see what the Bible📖 has to say:

✝ Ephesians 2:8 For it is by grace you have been saved, through faith – and this not from yourselves, it is the gift of God.

If Auntie K.T. were aboard Noah's ark,
she would have studied the bees.
Luckily, back then they wore long layered dresses
to protect their ankles and those knobby knees.
The bee is related to the wasp and the ant
and can make honey and also bees wax.
They feed on nectar and honey
and are naturally sweet and that's the facts.

≈≈≈◇≈≈≈

April ❶❷

(Day 103 of 366)

Let's see what the Bible📖 has to say:

† Exodus 23:28 I will send the hornet ahead of you to drive the Hivites, Canaanites and Hittites out of your way.

Jack and his father went deer hunting
and happened to see a buck with huge antlers.
They tried to figure out how many points he had,
but between the two of them, they ran out of fingers.
As they were performing their math skills,
the deer got tired of waiting,
so he took a walk down to the creek
and met a doe, which whom he was dating.
Antlers are used to protect the buck
or any other animal who grows them
from an attack by another critter
or to show the females that they are a gem.
They are made out of a substance
that is like our finger and toe nails.
They will continually grow and grow,
kind of like Prince Roderick's hunting tales.

April ❶❸
(Day 104 of 366)

Let's see what the Bible📖 has to say:

[†] Psalm 42:1 As the deer pants for streams of water, so my soul pants for you, O God.

Buddy was opening the mail at his work one day
and there were fifty envelopes from the same place.
A sticky not floated from his hands over the trash can
saying, "Go Green!", he could feel the red on his face.
We are supposed to take care of the earth
and not abuse the land and such,
but just *saying* catch phrases to be popular
is non-productive and *little* bit too much.

"Go Green!"

April ❶❹

(Day 105 of 366)

Let's see what the Bible📖 has to say:

† Numbers 35:33 " 'Do not pollute the land where you are. Bloodshed pollutes the land; and atonement cannot be made for the land on which blood has been shed, except by the blood of the one who shed it.'"

Chew-Chew, the middle child,
hopes that he gets a new baseball glove.
His parents have *their* hope in Jesus –
spending eternity with Him and everyone they love.

April ❶❺

(Day 106 of 366)

Let's see what the Bible📖 has to say:

† Romans 15:13 May the God of hope fill you with all joy and peace as you trust in Him, so that you may overflow with hope by the power of the Holy Spirit.

The General was asked what he was doing for Easter, which is a common question co-workers ask each other. Another thing that is common, is the very next question: "What day does it fall on this year, before I call Mother." The formula is the Sunday after the first full moon that comes on or after the first day of spring. The date can be as early as March 22ⁿᵈ or late as April 25ᵗʰ to honor Jesus Christ, our risen King!

1 †

April ❶❻

(Day 107 of 366)

Let's see what the Bible📖 has to say:

† John 3:16 For God so loved the world that He gave His one and only Son, that whoever believes in Him shall not perish but have eternal life.

Sara-Sara and Lanore were taking a walk.
They had to meet Mary Lu at her volleyball class.
They each had a pretty umbrella in their hand,
because they saw sprinkles through the pane of glass.
It started to pour and then trickled off
and Lanore asked Mary Lu a question or two...
"How did it rain on my little nose
when I was looking down at my shoe?!"
Whether it sprinkles, rains, pours,
drips, mists or leans towards a monsoon,
just be thankful that God gives us water
and it *may* be okay to be thankful for a balloon.

April ❶❼

(Day 108 of 366)

Let's see what the Bible has to say:

† Psalm 72:6 He will be like rain falling on a mown field, like showers watering the earth.

Jules drives to work each day,
which is the only way to go.
She makes sure she drives like a Christian,
because her bumper sticker says it's so.

April ❶❽
(Day 109 of 366)

Let's see what the Bible📖 has to say:

† Luke 6:31 Do to others as you would have them do to you.

Racism is a very ugly thing
that makes otherwise nice people, mean.
Most of the time the hatred is learned
from something they heard or have seen.
Kimberella learned that the theory of Evolution
has a lot to do with the problem.
If we evolved from a monkey,
then the whites want to rule the kingdom.
They think they are the superior race –
that they evolved the most throughout time.
If humans would realize God created *all* the races,
it would help squelch almost any future crime.

😃 ☺   ☺ 😃

April ❶❾

(Day 110 of 366)

Let's see what the Bible has to say:

⊤ Romans 2:11 For God does not show favoritism.

**The General learned while studying his Bible
that when Jesus comes, He will be in the eastern sky.
So if you see the Buckskin's son-in-law looking up
while in Super Store's parking lot, you'll know why.**

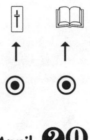

April ❷⓪

(Day 111 of 366)

Let's see what the Bible📖 has to say:

✝ Matthew 24:27 For as lightning that comes from the east is visible even in the west, so will be the coming of the Son of Man.

Chew-Chew's mommy read a story from the Bible.
Each page had a picture with animals of every sort.
Jules threw in that before the great Flood of Noah,
animals could have been bigger, causing him to snort.
He pictured a mousey the size of a puppy dog
and a puppy dog as big as a horse.
The thought of a horse the size of a dinosaur
was too much for him to imagine, of course.
There was a barrier of water around the earth
and it could possibly have been an ice ring.
It would have protected things, making them grow
like a tomato plant in a greenhouse during the spring.

April ❷❶
(Day 112 of 366)

Let's see what the Bible📖 has to say:

✝ **2 Samuel 21:20** In still another battle, which took place at Gath, there was a huge man with six fingers on each hand and six toes on each foot – twenty-four in all. He also was descended from Rapha.

Rochelle can picture being in Heaven,
thinking that it is too good to be true.
She'll wait for the other shoe to drop,
but it never, *ever* will in eternity for her or you!

FOREVER!

April ②②

(Day 113 of 366)

Let's see what the Bible📖 has to say:

✝ Luke 6:23 "Rejoice in that day and leap for joy, because great is your reward in Heaven. For that is how their fathers treated the prophets."

Baby No-No was walking behind her parents
at a Creation Science museum in Texas,
when she was told to watch where she was stepping,
so she didn't fall into a hole and make a big fuss.
The Paluxy River bed contains footprints together
of human beings and dinosaurs.
This is proof that the huge beasts lived with man –
was that just the sound of shutting doors?
Skeptics try to say that it is a hoax
or a Creation scientist is as loony as a bird.
Baby No-No may not know nothin',
but she's smart enough to believe in God's Word.

April ❷❸

(Day 114 of 366)

Let's see what the Bible📖 has to say:

✝ Job 40:15 "Look at the behemoth, which I made along with you and which feeds on grass like an ox."

Buddy wasn't born yesterday or even the day before,
so he has a hard time swallowing things that he reads.
Like the age of the earth and denial of the Flood...
he has to sort through the muck and pull out the weeds.
The size of the Mississippi Delta just doesn't add up,
when looking over the facts of the formation.
Going by the sediment accumulation that's divided,
it's under 30,000 years, just like our blessed nation.

≈≈≈≈≈≈

April ②④
(Day 115 of 366)

Let's see what the Bible📖 has to say:

✝ **Psalm 33:12** Blessed is the nation whose God is the Lord, the people He chose for His inheritance.

Jules went with her parents to the Passion Play
in South Dakota when she was just a teen.
Mr. and Mrs. Buckskin went to one in Arkansas
and it was the same, scene-by-scene.
They heard that it is also performed in Florida
when the winter gets a little cold up north.
If you get the chance to see this awesome display,
please don't head back home, but instead, go forth!

✝

April ②⑤
(Day 116 of 366)

Let's see what the Bible📖 has to say:

✝ Hebrews 13:8 Jesus Christ is the same yesterday and today and forever.

Jules was visiting Auntie K.T.
while she was on a business trip.
They took a tour of her yard
and Jules thought it was a kick.
She saw flowers hanging everywhere
and even dangling from the fence.
She could understand that location,
but the flowers on the clothesline made no sense.
She asked K.T. what her reasoning was
to place the flowers on the much-used line
and she cleared her throat to recite:
"To make sure they get plenty of sunshine.
I also want to make it easier
for the bees to pollinate the blossoms
and after their job is completed,
they can go to work on the possums."
Jules, who was confused at this statement,
wondered how possums made her black list.
"They like to eat them for a midnight snack,"
Auntie said and then shook her fist.
Jules helped her weed her garden,
trying to keep her happy and calm,
because truth be told, between you and me,
Jules likes to use violets as a soothing lip balm.
A sound like a helicopter was flying overhead,
going from basket to basket pollinating.
She then saw them go up a tree
and heard a squeal as they did their sting.

 buzzzzz...OUCH!

April ❷❻
(Day 117 of 366)

Let's see what the Bible📖 has to say:

✝ 1 Corinthians 15:55 "Where, O death, is your victory? Where, O death, is your sting?"

Jack and Sara-Sara were having a discussion that sometimes people go through suffering. In fact, we all do at some point in our lives. It may be to show others who is *our* King.

☹ ✝ ☺

April ②⑦

(Day 118 of 366)

Let's see what the Bible📖 has to say:

✝ **1** Peter 2:21 To this you were called, because Christ suffered for you, leaving you an example, that you should follow His steps.

Buddy heard the other day from a friend
that reptiles, as long as they live, will grow.
That means if they are meant to be a tall beast,
it will be a long way from their head to their toe.
Think about the 3-horned lizard that's around today,
living in pre-flood conditions under an ice ring.
That ring would block out the harmful sun
and it would grow up to be an animal king.
It doesn't have to be millions of years ago
to have the dinosaurs exist here on the earth.
Just special living conditions that have long since past
and Buddy thinks it was *thousands* of years' worth.

᛭

April ❷❽
(Day 119 of 366)

Let's see what the Bible📖 has to say:

† Job 41:8 If you lay a hand on him, you will remember
the struggle and never do it again!

Auntie K.T. likes to imagine
what Heaven will be like.
Will some people be elderly
while others are a little tyke?
If you look at it this way,
it seems a bit hard to gauge.
Why would we spend all of eternity as old or young?
Maybe, *just maybe*, we'll all be the same age.

April ❷❾

(Day 120 of 366)

Let's see what the Bible📖 has to say:

✝ Philippians 3:20 But our citizenship is in Heaven. And
we eagerly await a Savior from there, the Lord Jesus Christ,

Sara-Sara decided to teach her kids
about the camel's hump,
since it's an amazing design
to have fat stored in a lump.
The students were baffled,
since they thought the hump held water,
but she explained they store it
in their blood, just like they oughter.
They can use the stored fat
for up to two weeks of time.
And after that, it will go limp,
like a freshly squeezed lime.
After some rest, the empty hump
will fill back up with fat,
so when they go without food,
they can thank God for that.

∩ ∩

April **30**
(Day 121 of 366)

Let's see what the Bible📖 has to say:

🕆 Mark 10:25 "It is easier for a camel to go through the eye of a needle than for a rich man to enter the Kingdom of God."

Today when Rochelle read her Bible,
it talked about adultery.
This topic always makes her
feel a little queasy.
She learned over the years
that you have to trust your spouse,
but for some couples, not all,
this may *not* be entirely easy.

May ❶
(Day 122 of 366)

Let's see what the Bible has to say:

† Proverbs 6:32 But a man who commits adultery lacks judgment; whoever does so destroys himself.

Lanore was watching Grandpa Buckskin
swatting at flies with his fists.
She thought he was waving hello
without using either of his wrists.
She asked if flies come out of rotten meat
or if live animals attract them instead?
He replied that both are true of the pests
and bother you the most when you go to bed.
God created flies for a good reason
and Kimberella knows that for a fact.
They help clean up dead things
if they can avoid getting properly whacked.
It just *appears* that flies come out of meat,
because they lay their eggs atop a mess.
This is why when Grandma attends a picnic,
she covers her plate with the hem of her dress.

Shoo!

May ❷
(Day 123 of 366)

Let's see what the Bible📖 has to say:

✝ Isaiah 66:24 "And they will go out and look upon the dead bodies of those who rebelled against me; their worm will not die, nor will their fire be quenched, and they will be loathsome to all mankind."

Jack Sprat could eat no fat
at least that's how the nursery rhyme may go...
But *this* Jack can't digest the Big Bang theory,
because it could *never* happen – and even more so.

May ❸

(Day 124 of 366)

Let's see what the Bible📖 has to say:

☦ Genesis 1:1 In the beginning God created the heavens and the earth.

Did you ever try to type on a keyboard
that has a missing letter?
Or play a keyboard in a band with a note missing?
It's not that much better.
The result of missing information
is something that's not quite right.
Can you still hear or read it?
You may not *or* you just might.
Our bodies and brains
are wired like a computer,
only they have many more wires
and Kimberella things you will concur.
If just one nerve or organ
is damaged or taken away,
it could turn someone who is living
into someone who was once were.
(Was once were??)

May ❹
(Day 125 of 366)

Let's see what the Bible📖 has to say:

 Isaiah 26:19 But your dead will live; their bodies will rise, you who dwell in the dust, wake up and shout for joy. Your dew is like the dew of the morning; the earth will give birth to her dead.

Buddy says that the Rapture is coming.
Don't be one of those who will be left behind.
Ask God to forgive your sins and to be your Savior.
Live your life as a Christian and have peace of mind.
If you choose to ignore it and not take the steps,
you will suffer horribly for seven years.
For the ones left behind will have to choose
between Heaven and Hell, so do that now, my dears!

✝

May ❺
(Day 126 of 366)

Let's see what the Bible has to say:

⸸ John 12:48 There is a judge for the one who rejects me
and does not accept my words; that very word which I spoke
will condemn him at the last day.

One day in August, Baby No-No sat on a sidewalk.
She could feel the heat rising up through her diaper.
Her daddy was looking through a magnifying glass
to study the ants, so he could be absolutely sure.
How many legs do they have to carry heavy loads?
Who are the laborers and which one is the leader?
He held the glass a little closer for the baby to see
and what she saw was a few starting to teeter.
The Bible says we should study the ants
and we should listen to what God has to say.
Baby No-No learned along with her daddy
that the *best* time to view them is on a *cloudy* day....
(Just sayin')

May ❻
(Day 127 of 366)

Let's see what the Bible📖 has to say:

☦ Proverbs 6:6 Go to the ant, you sluggard; consider its ways and be wise!

**Prince Roderick took a correspondence course
to learn more about Evolution and Charles Darwin.
He wanted to understand why so many people choose
to use *that* theory so they can condone their sin.
He found out that it is pretty easy to understand why
they lean towards things coming about on their own,
because if *God* created everything, which He *did*,
they may have to change...did I just hear a moan?**

May ⑦
(Day 128 of 366)

Let's see what the Bible has to say:

☦ Romans 1:25 They exchanged the truth of God for a lie, and worshipped and served created things rather than the Creator – who is forever praised. Amen.

**Having three little children
and one big husband to boot,
Jules can sometimes feel like a servant
as she rushes around in a toot.
Jesus came as a servant
and we also need to be one as well.
No matter how busy life can get,
find time to serve others…Did I hear a dinner bell?!**

May ❽

(Day 129 of 366)

Let's see what the Bible📖 has to say:

† Luke 17:10 "So you also, when you have done everything you were told to do, should say, 'We are unworthy servants; we have only done our duty.'"

When Lanore first learned how to talk,
she decided to use her parents' language.
It was rather smart of her, of course,
to help them out…maybe just a smidge.
When man was first created,
God had them all speaking the same,
but then they built the Tower of Babel
and He saw it was like a children's game.
He scattered them across the miles
and confused their languages as well.
There are sixty-five hundred different ones today,
and *should* know the difference
between Heaven and Hell.

May ⑨
(Day 130 of 366)

Let's see what the Bible📖 has to say:

† Acts 2:8 Then how is it that each of us hears them in his own native language?

Chew-Chew is learning the difference
between trusting and testing.
He can choose to listen
to his parents or continue on.
If he trusts that they know
what is wrong or right,
he will not test them by doing things
while they are gone.
We all need to remember this
when God speaks to us.
If His holy Bible says
that something is so,
we trust in His Word
and live our lives accordingly.
Testing Him is disobedient
and NOT the way to go.

May **10**

(Day 131 of 366)

Let's see what the Bible has to say:

Hebrews 13:8 Jesus Christ is the same yesterday and today and forever.

If Sara-Sara were aboard Noah's ark,
she would have studied the horse.
How did they keep them harnessed up,
because running is their natural course?
The horse was domesticated by humans
a few thousand years ago.
They can sleep laying down or standing up
and use their speed to escape any foe.

≈≈≈⌂≈≈≈

May ❶❶

(Day 132 of 366)

Let's see what the Bible📖 has to say:

✝ **Proverbs 21:31** The horse is made ready for the day of battle, but victory rests with the Lord.

**Auntie K.T. wants to know
if you know who Jesus is.
He is God's Son. He is the Savior of the world.
Once saved, the Holy Spirit moves in and we are His!**

✝

May ❶❷

(Day 133 of 366)

Let's see what the Bible📖 has to say:

✝ John 14:26 But the Counselor, the Holy Spirit, whom the Father will send in my name, will teach you all things and will remind you of everything I have said to you.

The General believes the neck of a giraffe
had to be created and didn't evolve,
because something that's eighteen feet tall
would have to have had his problems solved.
How could he on his own figure out what is needed,
like and extra-large heart that's two feet long?
And a neck with a network of blood vessels,
so taking a drink wouldn't be considered wrong?
God knew how to help the magnificent giraffe out
by giving him extra-long legs to boot.
If he tried to evolve and gave himself short legs,
he would have had an awful time trying to root.

i

May ❶❸

(Day 134 of 366)

Let's see what the Bible📖 has to say:

☦ Revelation 4:11 "You are worthy, our Lord and God, to receive glory and honor and power, for you created all things, and by your will they were created and have their being."

Jules was reading Izzy Ann and Chew-Chew a book.
It was a story for little children about a new baby.
Their mommy stopped reading to think about a theory
that random molecules came together (not a maybe.)
Jules knows that there is nothing random about God –
He didn't use chance and either did the universe.
Besides, if we say that everything is random,
would even our thoughts be considered unrehearsed?

May ❶❹
(Day 135 of 366)

Let's see what the Bible📖 has to say:

† Psalm 94:11 The Lord knows the thoughts of man; He
know that they are futile.

Today when Auntie K.T. read her Bible,
it talked about happiness.
"This is easy," she said
as she stood up from her lawn chair.
"I will go water my flowers
and then weed my garden,
because working in my yard
brings me joy and some to spare."

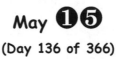

May ❶❺

(Day 136 of 366)

Let's see what the Bible has to say:

✝ Isaiah 12:3 With joy you will draw water from the wells of salvation.

**Witty Kitty went night crawler hunting
with Jack and Jules very late one night,
which was probably the right time to go,
since sunlight gives the creepy things fright.
Worms live in dirt, water, on plants or inside animals
and they crawl with no limbs to help them do so.
The creatures are part of our world's ecosystem,
so the cat opened the lid and let them all go.**

🐈 ~~~~~

May ❶❻

(Day 137 of 366)

Let's see what the Bible📖 has to say:

✝ Acts 12:23 Immediately, because Herod did not give praise to God, an angel of the Lord struck him down, and he was eaten by worms and died.

When Buddy was a young lad,
he used to climb up trees.
Now that he is older,
he just tries to save his knees.
When he takes a hike in the woods,
he absorbs the nature around him.
Trees are a multi-purpose plant
that can house birds in a nest on a limb.
Squirrels also call a tree their home,
especially ones that contain nuts.
Buddy says that if a *squirrel* is in a tree,
than it *must* and that's no ifs, ands or buts.
Some have flowers and others have fruit,
some provide materials to make boxes.
Sometimes they are cut down for firewood
or left standing to help shade the foxes.
No matter what a tree may mean to you,
thank God for designing them for us.
They're a joy to have all year long,
but the *fall* is when they cause the *most* fuss.

May ❶❼
(Day 138 of 366)

Let's see what the Bible📖 has to say:

☦ Job 14:7 "At least there is hope for a tree; If it is cut down, it will sprout again, and its new shoots will not fail."

Did you know that humans can make 10,000 expressions
from being absolutely giddy to
suffering from depression?
By using your eyes, nose, lips and forehead,
you can smile, frown, laugh or even play dead.
God designed each one of us to have certain emotions;
to use our organ of the face to relay
to others our notions.
Kimberella wants to see your beautiful smile –
That's it! Now please keep it going for just a little while.

☹ ☺ ☺

May ❶❽

(Day 139 of 366)

Let's see what the Bible📖 has to say:

✝ Proverbs 15:13 A happy heart makes the face cheerful, but heartache crushes the spirit.

**Jules and her mother were watching the children,
Izzy Ann, Chew-Chew and Baby No-No.
They were envious of their innocent playing –
to be like a child again someday would be a go!
Actually, God's Word says to have faith like a child,
as a newborn Christian to enter the Kingdom of God.
This includes: trusting, transparency, being carefree,
insistence, being spontaneous and smile as you nod.**

May ❶❾

(Day 140 of 366)

Let's see what the Bible has to say:

† Luke 18:17 I tell you the truth, anyone who will not receive the Kingdom of God like a little child will never enter it.

Fudgy wished he was designed to hibernate.
He thinks it sounds like a marvelous thing to do.
He pictures his body slowing its metabolism
and conserving energy by not even saying "boo!"
The part that sounds like it would be the most fun
is eating as much as he desires beforehand.
Then rest in a warm place and hide from the world
And "spring" back to life in his very own la-la land.

May **20**
(Day 141 of 366)

Let's see what the Bible📖 has to say:

⊤ Song of Songs 2:11 See! The winter is past; the rains are over and gone.

Witty Kitty turned to his Bible
to learn how to clean himself.
He got extremely dirty
when he climbed to the seventh shelf.
He turned to Leviticus,
since that's the book of laws
and in between turning the pages,
he licked his filthy paws.

May ②①
(Day 142 of 366)

Let's see what the Bible has to say:

 Leviticus 16:4 He is to put on the sacred linen tunic, with linen undergarments next to his body; he is to tie the linen sash around him and put on the linen turban. These are sacred garments; so he must bathe himself with water before he puts them on.

D.J. likes to collect rocks,
so precious stones would rock his boat.
Sometimes he has to take off his shoes and socks,
because in water, rocks and stones do not float.
Green is his very favorite color,
which of course would be an emerald,
although he wouldn't pass up a diamond
if he could dare to be so bold.
A sapphire of blue would go with his eyes
and gold could be used for a tooth,
but to hope that he also finds a jasper
may be considered just a tad bit uncouth.

◆◇◆◇◆◇◆◇

May ❷❷

(Day 143 of 366)

Let's see what the Bible📖 has to say:

✝ Ezekiel 28:13 You were in Eden, the garden of God; every precious stone adorned you: ruby, topaz and emerald, chrysolite, onyx and jasper, sapphire, turquoise and beryl, your settings and mountings were made of gold; on the day you were created they were prepared.

**Fudgy and Witty Kitty have a friend names Stretch.
He is a lizard that lives at the Critters R Us Zoo.
The duo decided to go visit him on the weekend.
They walked to his cage and asked, "What's new?"
"I think I grew an inch since you've seen me last,
because I'm a reptile and I'll grow until my last day."
Fudgy exclaimed, "That's what the dinosaur was!
In pre-flood conditions, it grew the behemoth's way!"**

🐈 🐈

May ❷❸
(Day 144 of 366)

Let's see what the Bible has to say:

† Proverbs 30:28 A lizard can be caught with the hand, yet it is in kings' palaces.

Sara-Sara was teaching her class
about the porcupine, who has needles like glass.
"If you see one, run the opposite way
or he will hurt you, but he's immune to his spray."
God knew what He was doing with the porcupine
when He designed the quills so sharp and fine.
He gave them a defense against his foe
and also for him...the get-up-and-go!

ᗰᗰ
ᗰᗰ

May ➋➍
(Day 145 of 366)

Let's see what the Bible📖 has to say:

† Job 14:22 He feels but the pain of his own body and mourns only for himself.

**Did you know that the planets spin
in all different directions *from* each other?
If there really *was* a Big Bang,
they should follow suit *with* one another.
If a merry-go-round filled with children
spun super-fast, causing them to fall,
even Mary Lu, who is only eight
knows they would fly the same way, big or small.**

May ➋➎
(Day 146 of 366)

Let's see what the Bible has to say:

Psalm 19:1 The heavens declare the glory of God; the skies proclaim the work of His hands.

Izzy Ann has a little Scottish in her...
about as much as a teaspoon in her elbow,
so when she heard about the Loch Ness Monster,
she loaded her backpack and was ready to go.
Jules took her to the local library,
for her to check out three or four books.
One contained a life-size photo,
needless to say, she got some funny looks.
Her mommy and daddy took turns reading to her
every night before she went to sleep.
Her dreams were of riding the back of her friend,
Nessie...the mild and the meek.

May ❷❻

(Day 147 of 366)

Let's see what the Bible📖 has to say:

✝ Ecclesiastes 5:7 Much dreaming and many words are meaningless. Therefore stand in awe of God.

**Prince Roderick has a hard time controlling himself
when he hears Evolution is how animals came about.
He can't picture Adam naming them one-by-one,
waiting millions of years to say, "A pig without a snout."**

Oink?

May ②⑦
(Day 148 of 366)

Let's see what the Bible📖 has to say:

☩ Proverbs 11:22 Like a gold ring in a pig's snout is a beautiful woman who shows no discretion.

Auntie K.T. was tending to her garden
and her neighbor asked her to come over the fence.
She wanted to show her the tomato plant
that she's growing... she couldn't stand the suspense.
She went inside of the woman's garage
and the plant was actually a tree!
It had tomatoes on it that were *huge*
and it's height, in feet, was over 63!
The woman explained she used special conditions
that probably resembled the earth before the Flood.
With a canopy of water that may have been ice,
things grew gigantic, including a tomato bud.
So imagine, if you will, lizards growing
along with everything else on this earth.
They grew all their lives, and probably lived longer;
they would become dinosaurs with tremendous girth.

←------------------------→

May ❷❽

(Day 149 of 366)

Let's see what the Bible has to say:

☨ **1** Corinthians 3:7 So neither he who plants nor he who waters is anything, but only God, who makes things grow.

**D.J. learned during a Bible study last week
that those who inherit the earth are the meek.
If you get mocked because of your belief,
don't cower or weep...but *rejoice*, giving a sigh of relief!**

Aaaaah....

May ❷❾
(Day 150 of 366)

Let's see what the Bible📖 has to say:

† **Psalm 37:11** But the meek will inherit the land and enjoy great peace.

Chew-Chew likes to throw a ball
all the way across the room.
Even though he's been cautioned
by his grandma peering over her loom.
"That ball is going so fast, it could break something!"
she cries out to her grandson in distress.
He just gives her one of his winning smiles,
trying to turn her mood into one of impress.
She thinks to herself as she weaves over and under
about what she heard about the world slowing down.
If the universe is as old as some people claim,
our globe would be stopped like a train in mid-town.

May ③⓪

(Day 151 of 366)

Let's see what the Bible📖 has to say:

† Psalm 104:5 He set the earth on its foundations; it can never be moved.

Rochelle tries to follow God's Word to the letter,
which means when eating fruit, also eat the seeds.
Scientists found out that they contain cyanide,
which could help fight cancer, like spraying weeds.

••

May ❸❶

(Day 152 of 366)

Let's see what the Bible📖 has to say:

☩ Genesis 1:29 Then God said, "I give you every seed-bearing plant on the face of the whole earth and every tree that has fruit with seed in it. They will be yours for food."

**Baby No-No was born today
and God knew her from the very start.
He didn't have to find out years later,
which way her hair would part.
He knew her while she was in the womb
and will continue to be totally in the know.
He'll know before Baby No-No would find out
whether she prefers sandy beaches or lots of snow.**

June ❶

(Day 153 of 366)

Let's see what the Bible📖 has to say:

✝ **Proverbs 2:10** For wisdom will enter your heart, and knowledge will be pleasant to your soul.

**Mary Lu was telling Lanore and Izzy Ann
that eclipses come in more than one kind.
She stated that there's a lunar and a solar,
depending if the moon goes in front or behind.
Did God make it this way for us to have a show
or is it just a result of His awesome Creation?
Mary Lu told her little sister and cousin,
"Probably both – practicality with a little bit of fun!"**

June ❷

(Day 154 of 366)

Let's see what the Bible📖 has to say:

✝ Joel 2:31 The sun will be turned to darkness and the moon to blood before the coming of the great and dreadful day of the Lord.

**Kimberella has a memory that has been compared –
to an elephant that makes her feel kind of sick.
If elephants' brains are more dense than humans',
how smart *exactly* is her husband, Prince Roderick?!**

?

June ❸

(Day 155 of 366)

Let's see what the Bible📖 has to say:

☦ Proverbs 10:7 The memory of the righteous will be a blessing, but the name of the wicked will not.

**Rochelle is *not* a perfectionist,
in fact, she is far from it.
She also knows that *nobody* is perfect
and only Jesus Christ will justly fit.
It doesn't mean we're not supposed to try
to live our lives like Jesus.
We just have to realize from the start
that perfect will *never* be an adjective for *us*.**

✝

June ❹

(Day 156 of 366)

Let's see what the Bible has to say:

⊤ James 3:2 We all stumble in many ways. If anyone is never at fault in what he says, he is a perfect man, able to keep his whole body in check.

Auntie K.T. went to her shed
to fetch a basket to hold the weeds.
She pulled with too much gusto
and then started to form sweat beads.
Kimberella watched in horror
and asked Auntie why she does it.
K.T. just shrugged her shoulders
and used some of her sharp wit:
"I think weeds deserve my attention,
just like the plants you see around me,
because if I ignore the least of these,
they'll grow and nothing else I'll see.
The weeds will demand my attention
and make me pull them out,
so I'd rather treat them as equals
as I'm making my rounds about."
If God didn't create weeds,
we may not appreciate the good.
We'd all become spoiled rotten
and not work as hard as we should.
Kimberella got on her knees
to help Auntie K.T. weed,
but she also said a prayer
to thank God for this need.

LL LL

June ❺

(Day 157 of 366)

Let's see what the Bible📖 has to say:

† Genesis 2:15 The Lord God took the man and put him in the Garden of Eden to work it and take care of it.

**Prince Roderick has a question for you,
so please listen closely, if you may:
"Do you know where you are going...
when it's time for the Judgement Day?"**

June ❻

(Day 158 of 366)

Let's see what the Bible📖 has to say:

✝ John 12:48 There is a judge for the one who rejects me and does not accept my words; that very word which I spoke will condemn him at the last day.

**Did you know that at one time
gorillas were thought to be a myth?
D.J. thinks this is what is
going on with Sasquatch.
There were stories of strong,
furry beasts in the forests
that were hard to believe
and even harder to watch.
Then one day
they were finally proven as real
and everyone knew
they were a type of monkey.
When someone *finally*
has proof of Big Foot,
they will be as commonplace
as a zoo's entrance fee.**

June ❼

(Day 159 of 366)

Let's see what the Bible📖 has to say:

✝ Jeremiah 23:24 "Can anyone hide in secret places so that I cannot see him?" declares the Lord. "Do not I fill Heaven and earth?" declares the Lord.

If the earth seems crowded to you where you live,
you may want to move to a different location.
Baby No-No doesn't know nothin',
but the babe *will* watch while on vacation.
Too many people in one area
may cause some human beings to think
that we need to control the population
with nothing more than a nod or a wink.
Baby No-No was in Wyoming
with her grandparents in the month of May
and what she saw was room galore
for her whole town to spread out and play.

June ❽

(Day 160 of 366)

Let's see what the Bible📖 has to say:

† Genesis 1:28 God blessed them and said to them, "Be fruitful and increase in number; fill the earth and subdue it. Rule over the fish of the sea and the birds of the air and over every living creature that moves on the ground."

**Today when Jules read her Bible,
it talked about love,
which is from God
and we *should* love one another.
Whoever loves
has been born of God,
so go over and give a hug
to your sister or your brother.**

XOXO

June ❾
(Day 161 of 366)

Let's see what the Bible📖 has to say:

✝ **1** John 4:7 Dear friends, let us love one another, for love has been born of God and knows God.

Fudgy has been mistaken as a bear
more that you can shake a stick at,
but if you really *do* see a bear up close,
throw your stick away and reach for a bat!
The wooly mammoths that were found frozen
at the North Pole, that is pretty much cold,
were found with food still in their stomachs,
which is strange if they were really old.
Could it be that they were quickly frozen
like during the onset of the great Flood?
Where an ice ring suspended above the earth
was hit while the beasts were chewing their cud?

Brrrrr

June ①⓪

(Day 162 of 366)

Let's see what the Bible📖 has to say:

† Job 26:10 He marks out the horizon on the face of the waters for a boundary between light and darkness.

If The General were aboard Noah's ark,
he would have studied the ants.
They would fall in line and march
right up the legs of his pants.
The ant is identified by an elbowed antennae –
there's queens, workers and soldiers.
They also have slender tiny waists,
whether they are the hims or the hers.

≈≈≈◻≈≈≈

June ❶❶

(Day 163 of 366)

Let's see what the Bible📖 has to say:

✝ Proverbs 6:6 Go to the ant, you sluggard, consider its ways and be wise!

Mary Lu was lying on her back
looking at the blue sky above her.
She saw a cloud drift by that was white,
but the name of it she was not sure.
She remembered Grandpa naming the clouds
as they rolled by all summer long,
but they have such difficult names,
that she made up her own little song:

I'll call that one Miss Fluffy,
because she is big and white.
That one's Mr. Doom,
'cause he could zap your kite.
Look out! Over there's a funnel,
its name is just plain Twister.
It can do a lot of damage
and could be a Miss or a Mister.
When the sky is blue and sunny,
it can be pretty boring,
but when it's dark and gloomy,
it can wake up daddy when he's snoring.

June ❶❷

(Day 164 of 366)

Let's see what the Bible📖 has to say:

✝ Proverbs 16:15 When a king's face brightens, it means life; his favor is like a raincloud in spring.

**Izzy Ann was told in school
to make up a family tree.
She decided to do it at home
to use her Bible so she can see.
She needed help lifting it on the bus,
so the driver jumped out to give her a hand.
She didn't start with her great grandpa,
she went back to the first man in the land.**

June ❶❸

(Day 165 of 366)

Let's see what the Bible📖 has to say:

✝ **1 Corinthians 15:45** So it is written: "The first man Adam became a living being", the last Adam, a life-giving spirit.

When Prince Roderick was a wee lad,
he wanted a pet skunk really bad.
His parents were reluctant, but gave in,
thus his frown turned into a grin.
He called his pet, Mister Stinky,
and held his nose over his binky.
The skunk sprayed everything in its way,
including his father's breakfast tray.
Prince Roderick was upset to the core
when his father showed Mr. Stinky to the door.
It's kind of neat that God designed certain critters
to protect themselves from getting the jitters.
Whatever mechanism they have to defend
also blocks *them* from the stuff that they send.

P.U.!

June ❶❹
(Day 166 of 366)

Let's see what the Bible📖 has to say:

✝ Revelation 21:4 "He will wipe every tear from their eyes. There will be no more death or mourning or crying or pain, for the old order of things has passed away."

Today when D.J. read his Bible,
it talked about perverse talk.
Before he became a Christian,
he needed his mouth washed out with soap.
Now when he hears someone else using
the same words he did as a teen,
he remembers the ugly words
and feels like a great big dope.

June ❶❺

(Day 167 of 366)

Let's see what the Bible📖 has to say:

† Ephesians 5:4 Nor should there be obscenity, foolish talk or coarse joking, which are out place, but rather thanksgiving.

Summer is warm and summer is hot.
The sun sure likes to shine a lot.
You can go to the store and not take a coat
or sail across water in a topless boat.
The garden is overflowing with zucchinis
as well as the beach with two-piece bikinis.
Autumn is cool and Autumn is warm.
Geese overhead are in good form.
You can squeeze in another campfire
or hike in the woods, if that's your desire.
The trees are full of colorful leaves.
Sweaters are worn in a variety of weaves.
Winter is cold and winter is bitter.
Indoor games are played with the sitter.
You can ice skate and drink hot cocoa
or sit by a fire for an hour or so.
You can see from your window a child's snowman
as you plan your trip where you can catch a tan.
Spring is refreshing and spring is wet.
Shoveling snow is no longer a threat.
You notice the days are getting longer
and your motivation is getting stronger.
Maybe you'll plant some new trees this year...
you can almost hear the birds give a cheer.
Kimberella wonders if God gave us each season
to make people understand their reason –
to go through life stage-by-stage with mirth:
Youth, middle age, old age and rebirth.

4 Seasons

June ❶❻
(Day 168 of 366)

Let's see what the Bible📖 has to say:

✝ Genesis 8:22 "As long as the earth endures, seed time and harvest, cold and heat, summer and winter, day and night will never cease."

Mary Lu turned to her Bible to learn about finances.
She scratched her head while trying to understand.
The Book of Hebrews said not to fall in love with money,
so she fed her piggy bank with her other hand.

June ❶❼

(Day 169 of 366)

Let's see what the Bible📖 has to say:

† **Hebrews 13:5** Keep your lives free from the love of money and be content with what you have, because God said, "Never will I leave you; never will I forsake you."

Fudgy thinks he's the smartest thing
on this side of the Mississippi.
That's pretty smart since the city of Dubuque
sits right on it and it's a long way to the sea.
Kimberella thinks that Adam must have been sharp
to have a vocabulary to name all the animals.
Think of the elephant and all the other bigs
down to the mouse and all of the smalls.

"Hippopotamus"

June ❶❽

(Day 170 of 366)

Let's see what the Bible📖 has to say:

✝ Genesis 2:19 Now the Lord God had formed out of the ground all the beasts of the field and all the birds of the air. He brought them to the man to see what he would name them; and whatever the man called each living creature, that was its name.

Lanore and her family went to Florida
and stopped to see Mickey and Minnie.
A lizard-type creature ran across the road
on the way to their hotel by the sea.
Sara-Sara suggested to her daughter
to get out her book from the library
to study about the reptile family
so she can identify it for free.
Here's what Lanore finally found out:
Reptiles will never stop growing,
which explains how under a canopy,
the dinosaur and dragon were king.

June ❶❾

(Day 171 of 366)

Let's see what the Bible📖 has to say:

✝ Job 3:8 May those who curse days curse that day, those who are ready to rouse Leviathan.

Jack was thinking what could be the best day ever.
Maybe receiving a new bike for a Christmas present.
The day he graduated from college is on the list,
being a first-time homeowner and giving up paying rent.
Getting married made Jack very happy to say the least,
then having two daughters made him delighted.
In comparison, Jack thinks that all these things together
could be the worst day in Heaven, truth be said.

June ②⓪

(Day 172 of 366)

Let's see what the Bible📖 has to say:

✝ **1 Corinthians 2:9** However, as it is written: "No eye has seen, no ear had heard, no mind has conceived what God has prepared for those who love Him."

**Jules sits in her lawn chair every night
to look up at the sky to see the big light.
She kept it up for thirty days
to see the moon go through its phase.
Sliver, quarter-moon, full-moon, half-moon –
Lucky Charms is her favorite (she went to get her spoon.)**

¼ ½ ¾ Full ☾

June ❷❶

(Day 173 of 366)

Let's see what the Bible📖 has to say:

✝ **1** Samuel 20:18 Then Jonathan said to David: "Tomorrow is the New Moon festival. You will be missed, because your seat will be empty."

Witty Kitty asked Fudgy one day,
"Do you have a brain that is functioning?"
Fudgy showed his teeth, not to smile,
but to let the silly cat know who was king.
"Of course I have a brain!
What kind of question is that?"
Witty Kitty made a note
and put it under his hat.
Brains can be very delicate
and they can keep loads of information.
They send signals over your whole body
and don't even take a break on vacation.
God must be an awesome electrician
to wire all of our parts to our brain.
To think that it came about all by chance
goes against His holy Word's grain.

$$2 + 2 = 4$$
$$God > 1$$

June ❷❷
(Day 174 of 366)

Let's see what the Bible📖 has to say:

† Colossians 3:2 Set your minds on things above, not on earthly things.

Baby No-No doesn't know nothin',
but one thing the babe *does* think...
caves were probably formed
during the Flood of the Big Drink.
You will hear from guides afar
telling you that the formations are ancient,
but you can grow a stalactite quickly
under a building dripping from a vent.
If you don't believe the infant,
look it up for yourself.
Search for the word "stalactite"
on the 'net or in a book from a shelf.

! ! ! ! ! !

🌢 🌢 🌢 🌢 🌢 🌢

June ❷❸

(Day 175 of 366)

Let's see what the Bible📖 has to say:

✝ Proverbs 25:2 It is the glory of God to conceal a matter; to search out a matter is the glory of kings.

"If you tell a big enough lie
and tell it frequently enough,
it will be believed," said Adolf Hitler.
Sara-Sara says, "Evolution is a BIG bluff!"

June ❷❹

(Day 176 of 366)

Let's see what the Bible📖 has to say:

✝ Proverbs 12:22 The Lord detests lying lips, but He delights in men who are truthful.

Imagine how intelligent
a person would have to be
if hundreds of years old
is the age of he or she.
Adam could name all the animals
when God asked it of him.
If Rochelle had to name the giraffe,
she probably would have felt dim.
Noah was about four hundred eighty years old
when he started to build the ark,
which would make him about six hundred
when his family had to embark.
We think we're really smart,
sometimes smarter than God.
Don't you think that's silly,
if not at least a little odd?

👁 M 🚫 > God!

June ❷❺
(Day 177 of 366)

Let's see what the Bible📖 has to say:

✝ Genesis 2:19 Now the Lord God had formed out of the ground all the beasts of the field and all the birds of the air. He brought them to the man to see what he would name them; and whatever the man called each living creature, that was its name.

**Prince Roderick listens to his book on tape
that contains the Bible from beginning to end.
He knows that Jesus really walked the earth
and should become everyone's best friend.
God, the Almighty, is the ultimate judge
and judge He *will* do to us all.
The Bible is His perfect Word –
do what He wants, no matter how great or small.**

June ②⑥

(Day 178 of 366)

Let's see what the Bible has to say:

† **1** Peter 4:17 For it is time for judgement to begin with the family of God; and if it begins with us, what will the outcome be for those who do not obey the gospel of God?

"Don't touch the stove, it's hot!"
hollered Jack to his daughter, Lanore.
"You'll burn your little fingertips
and trust me, they will be *really* sore."
She backed away when she saw a bombardier beetle,
while visiting family in the state of Florida.
They have fire that shoots out of their hind end
and can burn her toes while on a see-saw.
If the insect evolved, it would be quite a feat,
since a built-in mechanism is part of his bod.
It keeps him from burning himself,
while he blasts and enemy who's crossing the sod.

I...Ouch!

June ②⑦
(Day 179 of 366)

Let's see what the Bible📖 has to say:

✝ Hebrews 12:29 For our "God is a consuming fire."

Jules got clunked in the head by an apple
as she was reading a book under a tree.
She thought it was a colossal coincidence,
since meteorites were the subject, you see.
They originate from outer space,
which is a long way from the city park.
They're made of debris from comets
and when they strike earth, they can make a mark.
Why are there comets flying around space
when the so-called Big Bang of yesterday
happened billions and billions of years ago?
Shouldn't they all be by now fizzled away?
Meteorites make sense for a young universe,
because things are still settling down.
Look it up for yourself, starting with Genesis 1:1 –
"In the beginning" may alter your defiant frown.

?☹ ☺!

June ❷❽

(Day 180 of 366)

Let's see what the Bible has to say:

† Genesis 1:1 In the beginning God created the heavens
and the earth.

"Kimberella asks, "How big is your God?
Can He make the mountains and divide a sea?
Or is He tucked away on a shelf
where all you depend on is 'little 'ole me?'"
Mrs. Buckskin's God is not big...He's huge.
He knows what He wants the very first time.
We *all* need to fear Him and show Him praise
for giving us life, not costing us a single dime!

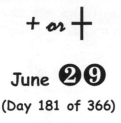

June ❷❾
(Day 181 of 366)

Let's see what the Bible📖 has to say:

✝ Revelation 1:8 "I am the Alpha and the Omega," says the Lord God, "who is, and who was, and who is to come, the Almighty."

Mary Lu studied emotions
in her Sunday School class last week.
The lesson was on feeling sad
and not wanting to even speak.
Her teacher told the class
if this is ever something that they feel,
to try imagining something happy
that would make them give a squeal.
God designed us with so many emotions
that are needed to be the human beings we are.
Anyone can see a smile or when someone is crying –
from any nation on earth close by or from afar.

☹   ☺

June 30

(Day 182 of 366)

Let's see what the Bible📖 has to say:

✝ Proverbs 15:18 A hot-tempered man stirs up dissension, but a patient man calms a quarrel.

**If Izzy Ann feels a little sick
like a fever and a tummy ache,
she knows that her immune system is kicking in
so she'll get better to help her mommy bake.
Jules knows it's a pretty elaborate procedure
to have happened on its own.
Do you think that God designed it that way
or it came from somewhere unknown?**

July ❶

(Day 183 of 366)

Let's see what the Bible has to say:

✝ James 5:14 Is any one of you sick? He should call the elders of the church to pray over him and anoint him with oil in the name of the Lord.

Were we *born* a Christian?
We may have been born into family
that are Christians or think that they are,
but it takes more than birth for us to be.
Kimberella says to be a *true* Christian
is a choice that each person has to make.
We claim Jesus as our Savior
and repent, then we will awake!

July ❷
(Day 184 of 366)

Let's see what the Bible📖 has to say:

✝ Romans 10:10 For it is within your heart that you believe and are justified, and it is with your mouth that you confess and are saved.

Did it rain before the Flood?
The General scratched his head.
Maybe the canopy that circled the earth
provided the needed moisture instead.

July ❸
(Day 185 of 366)

Let's see what the Bible📖 has to say:

✝ Genesis 7:4 "Seven days from now I will send rain on the earth for forty days and forty nights, and I will wipe from the face of the earth every living creature I have made."

How many of you heard of fish flies?
Lanore will do her best not to gag.
They appear on the Mississippi River
about the time they wave the 4th of July's flag.
The *good* news is they don't last long,
but when they arrive, they put up a stink.
Cars will get in wrecks when they slide
on the bridge that goes over the Big Drink.

≈≈≈≈≈≈

July ❹

(Day 186 of 366)

Let's see what the Bible📖 has to say:

✝ Leviticus 11:20 'All flying insects that walk on all fours are to be detestable to you.'

Rochelle read an article
that over fifty million babies were aborted,
which has been from the year
Nineteen Seventy-Three.
That's a hundred million people
that could have adopted.
She put down her paper and wondered,
"When will they *ever* see?"
A baby is a person
the second of conception,
not just a blob of tissue
that *some* want you to believe.
We can *all* have the privilege
to argue this point,
because *our* mothers chose *for* us
to *stay* and *not* to leave!

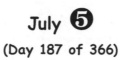

July ❺

(Day 187 of 366)

Let's see what the Bible has to say:

† Ecclesiastes 11:5 As you do not know the path of the wind, or how the body is formed in a mother's womb, so you cannot understand the work of God, the Maker of all things.

Auntie K.T. decided to raise some homing pigeons
and lined up their cages in a nice neat row.
When the Buckskins came to visit her,
Kimberella was thrilled, since her bats scared her so.
K.T. explained that the birds were used in wartime
and can fly fifty to ninety miles per hour.
They also have been recorded to wing it
up to 1,100 miles back home to take a shower.
This information was interesting to Mrs. Buckskin,
because she thinks keeping clean is a must.
To her a dirty bird is one that swoops overhead
and takes her bobby pins along with her trust.
"Bye-Bye Auntie K.T. – until we meet again.
Which way is home?!" K.T. cried, "Head west."
On the way home, Kimberella asked her prince,
"Do homing pigeons really *ever* leave the nest?"

July ❻
(Day 188 of 366)

Let's see what the Bible📖 has to say:

✝ Matthew 6:26 Look at the birds of the air; they do not sow or reap or store away in barns, and yet your heavenly Father feeds them. Are you not much more valuable than they?

The General had to pick up a snake
that he found in the yard by the garden.
He didn't want to have to touch it,
but he couldn't have Jules' heart harden.
He explained to his three adorable children
that snakes will shed their skin and grow anew.
Jules poked her head out the back screen door
and when she saw it, she screamed, "EEEWWW!"
A snake can slither through a doorway
and some will even climb up a tree.
In Eve's case in the Garden of Eden,
he talked to her as an enemy.

"You will certainly not die."

July ❼
(Day 189 of 366)

Let's see what the Bible📖 has to say:

† Genesis 3:1 Now the serpent was more crafty than any of the wild animals the Lord God had made. He said to the woman, "Did God really say, you must not eat from any tree in the garden?"

**Today when Mary Lu and Lanore read their Bible,
it talked about purity.
Then Mary Lu told her sister
"Let no one despise you for your youth.
Also, set the believers an example
in speech, in conduct and love.
Also, in faith and in purity" –
Lanore smiled showing her missing tooth.**

July **8**

(Day 190 of 366)

Let's see what the Bible has to say:

1 Timothy 4:12 'Don't let anyone look down on you because you are young, but set an example for the believers in speech, in life, in love, in faith and in purity.'

God gave us free will, so we can do the choosing.
We can decide to have the side of winning or losing.
He *could* have designed us like robots who will follow...
worshipping God, behaving kindly and never wallow.
He didn't. He wants us to love Him on our own accord
like if Prince Roderick only had friends he can afford.
It wouldn't make him feel better
because he paid them to,
so please make choices benefitting
the Almighty and you.

FREE!

July ❾

(Day 191 of 366)

Let's see what the Bible📖 has to say:

† Joshua 24:15 "But if serving the Lord seems undesirable to you, then choose for yourselves this day whom you will serve, whether the gods your forefather served beyond the River, or the gods of the Amorites, in whose land you are living. But as for me and my household, we will serve the Lord."

D.J. was in church last week
and baptism was the sermon.
For babies they call it a dedication
whenever they have it done.
You don't have to be baptized –
God saves you without it,
but even Jesus had it done
by John whom He deemed as fit.

≈≈≈≈≈≈

July ❶⓪

(Day 192 of 366)

Let's see what the Bible📖 has to say:

✝ Mark 16:16 Whoever believes and is baptized will be saved, but whoever does not believe will be condemned.

**If Izzy Ann, Chew-Chew and Baby No-No
were aboard Noah's ark,
they would have all studied behemoth,
in other words the dinosaur.
Noah could have just picked out sets
of babies to make them smaller,
so that way, balancing the boat
wouldn't have been a chore.
The behemoth is just
another word for dinosaur.
The word "dinosaur"
wasn't invented until 1842.
They were just lizards
blown up to monster size,
because of a canopy
that was over the skies of blue.**

≈≈≈◇≈≈≈

July ❶❶
(Day 193 of 366)

Let's see what the Bible has to say:

✝ Job 40:15 "Look at the behemoth, which I have made along with you and which feeds on grass like an ox."

D.J. tries to give signals to the other members
when 'Jack and The Old Folk Band' have a gig.
He'll wave his hand and nod his head
and is even known to make his eyes look *really* big.
How did language just happen to evolve?
Did someone have a thought that needed to get out?
Then had to go back to the drawing board,
so the next generation can give a shout?
To D.J., it's just plain for him to see
that everyone has a desire to communicate.
Even someone who is deaf will use his hands,
so he doesn't miss out and have to wait.

July ❶❷

(Day 194 of 366)

Let's see what the Bible📖 has to say:

✝ Genesis 11:6 The Lord said, "If as one people speaking the same language they have begun to do this, then nothing they plan to do will be impossible for them."

**Witty Kitty was at pet daycare
playing with a calico cat named Groove.
His attitude is that he *would* be a team player
If someone *else* would make the first move.**

🐈 *Stale Mate!* 🐈

July ❶❸
(Day 195 of 366)

Let's see what the Bible📖 has to say:

✝ Romans 14:1 Accept him whose faith is weak, without passing judgment on disputable matters.

The General wants to know if you ever thought
what would a person do if he couldn't think.
Would he just walk across the kitchen floor
and put his mouth to the faucet at the sink?
No, because it would take thought to do such a thing
and the kitchen designer would
have had to use *their* brain.
The General wants to know how
did the ability of thinking
evolve from nothing to taking a
walk down Memory Lane.
He concluded that God gave us the power of thought
to make choices to survive in this world,
so please take the time to use your noggin
and read God's Word (even the pages that have curled.)

July ❶❹

(Day 196 of 366)

Let's see what the Bible has to say:

† Proverbs 15:28 The heart of the righteous weighs its answers, but the mouth of the wicked gushes evil.

Jack was walking at the zoo
with Sara-Sara, Lanore and Mary Lu.
He was telling them during their trot
whether a critter practices migration or not.
The zebra, gazelle and wildebeest
will roam while they partake in a feast,
while the insects, birds and bats
fly to places where people wear different hats.
God put the sense of direction into His Creation,
so they can proceed with the process of migration.
Mary Lu asked her daddy which way to walk next.
Sara-Sara pointed as she saw hubby sending a text.
A natural GPS that God designed is easier to follow
than the theory of Evolution, which is hard to swallow.

July ❶❺
(Day 197 of 366)

Let's see what the Bible📖 has to say:

✝ Genesis 7:15 Pairs of all creatures that have the breath of life in them came to Noah and entered the ark.

Jules was reading her favorite book
on her porch that sits in the back.
All of a sudden out of nowhere,
a lightning bolt appeared and she heard a crack.
The porch's light went out
and so did the rest of the house.
She reached for her cell phone
that was in a pocket of her blouse.
Her husband, The General,
tried to calm his wife down
by telling her to get a flashlight
and put on her nightgown.
He said, "I know you don't like thunderstorms
since you've been little,
but without electricity you can forget your book,
so just relax and play your fiddle.

July ❶❻
(Day 198 of 366)

Let's see what the Bible📖 has to say:

† Matthew 24:27 For as lightning that comes from the east is visible even in the west, so will be the coming of the Son of Man.

Grandpa Buckskin decided to show Lanore
a few things he put in his sock.
There was a watch, stick, daffodil,
and a baseball-sized rock.
"Reach in there and draw one out,"
he asked of his little tot.
She pulled out first the flower
and he asked her, "God-made or not?"
Even at three years old, Lanore knew the answer:
"God-made," she squealed and gave a little smile.
She said the same for the stick and the rock.
"Not!" she cried out for the timepiece with a dial.
Prince Roderick thinks that if a three year old
can plainly see the difference,
than why do adults who study long and hard
insist that they stay sitting on the fence?

July ①⑦
(Day 199 of 366)

Let's see what the Bible📖 has to say:

✝ Job 12:9 "Which of all these does not know that the
hand of the Lord has done this?"

Let's talk about gases
that make up our world.
Like: Nitrogen, Oxygen, Helium
and Methane, just to name a few.
How are we supposed to believe
that they just happened to form?
Jules doesn't buy "chance" –
she just knows that *her* God knew.

Got a match?

July ❶❽
(Day 200 of 366)

Let's see what the Bible📖 has to say:

✝ Job 26:7 He spreads out the northern skies over empty space; He suspends the earth over nothing.

When the cuckoo bird cuckoos, announcing Nine O'clock
and Big Bird welcomes Chew-Chew to Sesame Street,
Liberty bird, in his cage hanging from the ceiling,
puts in his two cents by speaking through his feet:
"Hello down there! Can you turn the volume up?
I want to learn my numbers and alphabet."
Since the cuckoo bird had to wait a half hour,
Chew-Chew answered *for* him, "You're a silly pet!
You're just a bird that can repeat things,
not a creature that can read and comprehend."
Liberty bird opened his cage and flew to the ground
with his parachute landing on the armchair's bend.
He nudged Chew-Chew out of his way,
and walked to the remote to turn up the volume.
"Listen here!" he said as he nailed shut the clock's door.
"I'm the cutest, smartest bird that's been in this room!"
Did God create birds that can talk to keep us in line?
To make us look around and think before we speak.
"A little birdie told me," may not be so far-fetched
when you take a gander at this
verse...so watch your beak!

July ①⑨
(Day 201 of 366)

Let's see what the Bible📖 has to say:

✝ Ecclesiastes 10:20 Do not revile the king even in your thoughts, or curse the rich in your bedroom, because a bird of the air may carry your words, and a bird on the wing may report what you say.

**Baby No-No turned to her Bible
to learn about eating.
She couldn't read yet,
but her mommy helped her out.
The Book of Isaiah talks about
eating curds and honey –
if you refuse evil
and choose good to be your route.**

July **20**

(Day 202 of 366)

Let's see what the Bible📖 has to say:

✝ Isaiah 7:15 He will eat curds and honey when he knows enough to reject the wrong and choose the right.

Let's talk about Noah's ark,
which is Buddy's favorite subject.
He doesn't like it when he hears the argument
that to sail, it's too big of an object.
Buddy thinks that God's intentions were
to just have the boat anchored down
and *not* to sail the ark *anywhere*,
but only to float, so they all wouldn't drown.

≋≋≋◻≋≋≋

July ❷❶
(Day 203 of 366)

Let's see what the Bible📖 has to say:

✝ **Genesis 7:18** The waters rose and increased greatly on the earth, and the ark floated on the surface of the water.

Jack was asked one day at work
why he doesn't drive an electric car.
He pondered over that one for half a day
and put the idea into a jar.
Sara-Sara had him reach in and draw one out
to see what he would do one afternoon.
When he pulled out to shop for some wheels,
he sat in his gas-powered car to fume.
"If I have to plug into the wall
every night when I park my car,
I can see me forgetting to *unplug*
and to my shock, won't be able to go far.
I'll just stick to filling up a tank
about every week or two,
until the price of gasoline
costs more than buying brand new."

July ②②

(Day 204 of 366)

Let's see what the Bible📖 has to say:

✝ 2 Kings 9:20 The lookout reported, "He has reached them, but he isn't coming back either. The driving is like that of Jehu son of Nimshi – he drives like a madman."

The General went to his Bible study
that's held every Monday night.
This week's lesson was the Ten Commandments
and everyone sat up straight to listen tight.
God, with his finger wrote them on tablets
and sent Moses on his way,
but Moses got angry at some people
and broke them to his dismay.
God had to write them again
and Moses tried it once more.
Here is what the tablets contained –
how we should live is what they are for:
No other gods before Him
No idols of any kind
Don't use His name in vain
The Sabbath you must keep in mind
Honor your mother and father
You shall not kill another
You shall not commit adultery
Don't steal at all, that means you too, brother
You shall not give false testimony
Don't covet your neighbor's wife
Keep all of these Ten Commandments
And you'll live a good, clean life.

July ❷❸
(Day 205 of 366)

Let's see what the Bible📖 has to say:

✝ Deuteronomy 4:13 He declared to you His covenant, the Ten Commandments, which He commanded you to follow and then wrote them on two stone tablets.

Izzy Ann and her mommy
went swimming in the sea.
The water was up to Izzy's chin
and just over Jules' knee.
The little girl got salt in her mouth
and promptly spit it out.
Jules questioned her daughter
why she decided to pout.
"The ocean tastes like a potato chip,
only wet and not dry.
When I dunk my head under the water,
my eyes begin to cry."
Her mommy took her hand
and walked her back to shore,
thinking, *"If the world is billions of years old,*
there would be much, much more."

July ②④

(Day 206 of 366)

Let's see what the Bible has to say:

† James 3:12 My brothers, can a fig tree bear olives, or a grapevine bear figs? Neither can a salt spring produce fresh water.

When God created the peacock
with his pretty feathers of teal,
Mary Lu is pretty sure that He did it
to show off His awesome creating zeal.
The tail of this magnificent bird
would be a hindrance to let him fly.
How could something that big and delicate
have the ability to go from low to high?

↕?

July ❷❺
(Day 207 of 366)

Let's see what the Bible📖 has to say:

† Isaiah 31:5 "Like birds hovering overhead, the Lord Almighty will shield Jerusalem; He will shield it and deliver it, He will 'pass over' it and will rescue it."

Here is the definition of macro-evolution:
"Major changes from one organism to another."
This of course, takes long periods of time –
to *this* theory, Kimberella says, "Oh, brother!"
Most people used to read their Bibles
and never heard of such malarkey,
but some are so distracted by toys and noise
that they have, on their own, *acted* like a monkey.
If you don't believe in long periods of time,
like millions and billions of years for instance,
you're considered an ignorant savage...
Mrs. Buckskin is one, she'll admit it without a wince.
She can stretch her brain to think of a lot of silly things,
like making a piece of gum taste like mashed potatoes,
but believing in things making big changes on their own
makes her laugh until milk comes out of her nose.
Let's take a ridiculous idea
that something crawled onto shore,
grew legs to walk across the beach,
then sprinkle it with a pinch or more.
That magic dust is eons of time –
too much for your poor brains to handle,
so instead of spending much time thinking,
they count on you snuffing out the candle.
Kimberella would like everyone to think
about reading their Bibles like their kin folk did...
and maybe, just maybe, the schools will change
by taking Evolution by the elbow to get rid.

July ②⑥

(Day 208 of 366)

Let's see what the Bible📖 has to say:

✝ Colossians 2:8 See to it that no one takes you captive through hollow and deceptive philosophy, which depends on human tradition and the basic principles of this world rather than on Christ.

Which came first, the heart or the blood?
Buddy says, "Neither is the answer.
If one came before the other one did,
the system wouldn't work that's for sure."
The heart is just one example that needs the fluid.
All the organs need it and other parts, too.
The precious blood has to keep flowing
inside of Buddy *and* inside of you!

♥

July ❷❼

(Day 209 of 366)

Let's see what the Bible has to say:

† Leviticus 17:11 For the life of a creature is in the blood, and I have given it to you to make atonement for yourselves on the altar; it is the blood that makes atonement for one's life.

When Baby No-No learned how to crawl,
her mommy let her go into the back yard.
Jules wanted to hang out some clothes,
but also doubled as a prison guard.
"Stay by me, little babe, and don't leave my sight!
Don't go over there or you will surely get hurt!
Look out! Here comes the neighbor's puppy!
You just smeared mud on my brand new shirt!"
When reaching for sun-screen to rub on her baby,
Kimberella told her daughter that it's *suntan* lotion.
"That's so old-school!" Jules scolded her mother,
"You don't *attract* rays, you are to *block out* the sun."
"Maybe that's why my skin looks like leather
and I have all these spots on my arms and back."
"No doubt," Jules said exasperated.
She then sent Mrs. Buckskin inside to pack.

July ❷❽

(Day 210 of 366)

Let's see what the Bible📖 has to say:

† Ecclesiastes 1:5 The sun rises and the sun sets, and hurries back to where it rises.

Kimberella and Prince Roderick
were baptized as little babies.
As adults, they *chose* on their own
to get fully submersed.
The first time is considered more of a dedication
to be raised by Godly parents.
As adults, to show obedience –
to Jesus who took their sins and purged.

≈≈≈≈≈

July ②⑨
(Day 211 of 366)

Let's see what the Bible📖 has to say:

† Acts 22:16 'And now what are you waiting for? Get up, be baptized and wash your sins away, calling on His name.'

Mary Lu does not like bugs,
especially an eight-legged spider.
You would hear her scream two states over
if one happened to sit down beside *her*.
She learned in school that they spin a web,
which looks like the tatting of fine lace.
That's okay if she's watching a documentary
and doesn't have one in the woods by her face.
Her sister, Lanore, asked Mary Lu a question,
which went something like this:
"Do you think that an octopus in the ocean
creeps out the mermaids as they swim, big Sis?"

July 30
(Day 212 of 366)

Let's see what the Bible📖 has to say:

✝ Deuteronomy 7:21 Do not be terrified by them, for the Lord your God, who is among you, is a great and awesome God.

Jack was trying to take a measurement
to figure out the distance from Earth to the moon.
That was hard enough for him to accomplish,
especially since he had to put down his spoon.
He was wondering how they can measure starlight
when the distance is hard to fathom.
When believing the universe is billions of years old, do
scientists make the results *fit* the desired outcome?

July ❸❶
(Day 213 of 366)

Let's see what the Bible📖 has to say:

✝ Job 22:12 "Is not God in the heights of Heaven? And
see how lofty are the highest stars!"

The General was put on dusting duty
while his wife busied herself with dishes.
He wiped down all of the furniture
and even the tank that held the fishes.
One week later, Jules handed him a cloth
and asked him to do it all again.
He couldn't believe his ears or eyes
and felt his head begin to spin.
"Where does all the dust come from?"
he yelled and was promptly hushed.
The children were all taking their naps,
thus his ideas of playtime were crushed.
After he was done (for that week anyway),
he looked on the internet to find an answer
about what dust really consists of.
He was pretty disgusted as he was telling her:
"Blowing dirt, bacteria, pollen and molds,
fibers and animal dander, that are on top of the bed.
Decomposing insects, dryer lint and hair,
dust mites and mostly our skin flakes that we shed."
They both gave a shutter and turned off the light
and laid in bed for hours with their eyes opened wide.
Now each morning when Jules makes the coffee,
hubby is dusting everywhere, including his *own* hide.

 Achoo!

August ❶
(Day 214 of 366)

Let's see what the Bible📖 has to say:

✝ Genesis 3:19 "By the sweat of your brow you will eat your food until you return to the ground, since from it you were taken; for dust you are and to dust you will return."

Lanore likes to play a copy cat
with her older sister, Mary Lu.
If she smacks a ball with a bat,
she grabs it and cries out, "Me too!"
In preschool, she learned just a bit
about carbon dating of a stone.
She got her bloomers in a snit,
'cause carbon should be used on a bone.
The teacher said that Carbon 14, she fears,
should only be used on things that were alive
and is only accurate for thousands of years,
not millions or billions and that's no jive!

5.25 trillion years old?!

August ❷
(Day 215 of 366)

Let's see what the Bible📖 has to say:

† Proverbs 19:5 A false witness will not go unpunished, and he who pours out lies will not go free.

Chew-Chew turned to his Bible to learn about working,
which is very hard to do since he was only two.
2 Thessalonians says if a man won't work, he won't eat.
He ran to his daddy and asked him what he can do.

August ❸

(Day 216 of 366)

Let's see what the Bible📖 has to say:

✝ **2** Thessalonians 3:10 For even when we were with you, we gave you this rule: "If a man will not work, he shall not eat."

Auntie K.T. swung into town
in her car and not on a vine.
Although, with her love of the outdoors,
she could have swung here just fine.
She went to Jules' house to see her garden,
but when she arrived her feelings were hurt.
Her niece was too busy with the children
to plant anything impressive in the dirt.
She set aside her feelings and said with a chirp,
"Let me help you plant some tomatoes
and if I am allowed by you to do so,
I'll throw in some herbs with the potatoes."
She grabbed a trowel and went to work
planting plenty of oregano for spaghetti.
Next was some garlic to go with it
along with mint saying, "One for them and two for me."
For brats and sauerkraut, she sowed caraway
and lavender for a long bubble bath.
She couldn't count the times Witty Kitty asked for catnip,
because she just didn't have the *thyme* to do the math.
Herbs didn't evolve, God created each on purpose.
Some help flavor our food to taste better,
while others have healing effects that can calm us.
Dill can do both if it's placed in a chunk of cheddar.
When Auntie K.T. decided that her job was complete,
she walked stooped over to her car.
Luckily, she didn't have to use a vine,
because with her back out, she wouldn't swing very far.

$\mathcal{U}$

August ❹

(Day 217 of 366)

Let's see what the Bible📖 has to say:

✝ Exodus 12:8 That same night they are to eat the meat roasted over the fire, along with bitter herbs, and bread made without yeast.

The General knows whether it's day or night.
by looking up at the sky to see if there's a light.
Sometimes he sees both the moon and the sun,
so he's confused whether to walk or run.
A sunny day is perfect to jog on the sidewalks...
a moonlit night is for strolling through corn stalks.
He decided to do both for just a little while.
Izzy Ann and Chew-Chew followed him in single file.

☾⋆ ✹

August ❺

(Day 218 of 366)

Let's see what the Bible has to say:

⊤ 1 John 1:7 But if we walk in the light, as He is in the light, we have fellowship with one another, and the blood of Jesus, His Son, purifies us from all sin.

**Prince Roderick gets upset
when some religions teach the following:
That Jesus wasn't the Son of God –
"HE *IS* THE SON OF GOD!!" he ends up hollering.**

August ❻

(Day 219 of 366)

Let's see what the Bible📖 has to say:

✝ Psalm 2:7 I will proclaim the decree of the Lord: He said to me, "You are my Son; today I have become your Father."

Do you believe that the Bible is true
and not just a book of fables?
Or do you believe in just yourself
having a good ole time around your table?
D.J. knows there are no contradictions –
each verse was very well thought out.
God inspired those men to write it,
so please choose to *believe* and *not* to doubt.

Yes or No?

August ❼

(Day 220 of 366)

Let's see what the Bible📖 has to say:

✝ 2 Peter 1:16 We did not follow cleverly invented stories when we told you about the power and coming of our Lord Jesus Christ, but we were eyewitnesses of His Majesty.

Kimberella's gift is to be organized,
Prince Roderick's is fixing things.
Jack's talent is to make guitars,
Sara-Sara's is when she sings.
Mary Lu's gift is to be helpful,
Lanore is finding candy.
Jules' talent is guiding others,
The General is to be handy.
Izzy Ann's gift is giving a smile,
Chew-Chew is to grow big feet.
Baby No-No's talent is to sleep,
D.J. knows how to keep a beat.
Buddy's gift is finding his way,
Rochelle's is listening to her friend.
Auntie K.T.'s talent is raising bats,
Fudgy is sitting on his hind end.
Witty Kitty's talent is always remembering
that *God* gave them, as He gives us *everything*.

August ❽
(Day 221 of 366)

Let's see what the Bible📖 has to say:

✝ James 1:17 Every good and perfect gift is from above, coming down from the Father of the heavenly lights, who does not change like shifting shadows.

When Baby No-No ages a couple more years
and she is beyond wearing diapers and crying tears,
she will learn to say her prayers before bedtime
and hopefully she won't find the need to rhyme.
When praying, you can actually talk right to God
you don't need someone interceding in a pod.
In fact, God knows what you need before you do...
this will help the babe her whole life through.

Amen!

August ➒

(Day 222 of 366)

Let's see what the Bible📖 has to say:

✝ Matthew 6:6 "But when you pray, go into your room, close the door and pray to our Father, who is unseen. Then your Father, who sees what is done in secret, will reward you."

Noah's ark could have been bigger
than we could ever imagine.
God told him how big to make it using cubits
and it was probably more thicker than thin.
However, The General thinks that humans
were a lot bigger back then, and he's talking tall,
because of the water barrier suspended around Earth
before the rains started to fall.
A cubit measures from your elbow
to the tip of your middle digit.
No matter what size your arm is
or whether you stand or prefer just to sit.
So imagine if you were to build a box
using your arm as a guide –
now picture the Jolly Green Giant
who's at least twice as high and wide.
The boxes would be a lot different in size,
thus proving The General's point...
that Noah could have fit a lot more animals
on a super-scale zoo-like joint!

August ❶⓪
(Day 223 of 366)

Let's see what the Bible📖 has to say:

† 2 Chronicles 4:2 He made the Sea of cast metal, circular in shape, measuring ten cubits from rim to rim and five cubits high. It took a line of thirty cubits to measure around it.

Today when Jack read his Bible,
it talked about justice.
If you've been wronged,
never avenge with words or sword.
Leave it to the wrath of God,
for it is written:
"Vengeance is mine,
I will repay says the Lord."

August ①①

(Day 224 of 366)

Let's see what the Bible📖 has to say:

✝ Romans 12:19 Do not take revenge my friend but leave room for God's wrath, for it is written, "It is mine to avenge; I will repay," says the Lord.

If Mary Lu and Lanore were aboard Noah's ark,
they would have studied the peacock.
In arts and crafts they would each make wings
and the three of them would become a flock.
The peacock is related to the pheasant
and has a distinct piercing call.
Its tail is called a train with eye spots
and it doesn't fly, but glides, so it doesn't fall.

≈≈≈◇≈≈≈

August ❶❷

(Day 225 of 366)

Let's see what the Bible📖 has to say:

✝ Psalm 104:24 How many are your works, O Lord! In wisdom you made them all; the earth is full of your creatures.

Chew-Chew may be small, age-wise that is,
but he knows when his soda pop gives a fizz –
to thank God for answering his prayer that day
and when he asks, he says, "Please, if you may."

✝

August ❶❸

(Day 226 of 366)

Let's see what the Bible has to say:

✝ Psalm 28:7 The Lord is my strength and my shield; my heart trusts in Him, and I am helped. My heart leaps for joy and I will give thanks to Him in song.

Witty Kitty thinks it's pretty silly
when he sees pets sporting a sweater.
God created the animals with fur
that suits them much, much better.
Their fur was designed to keep them warm
and also cool, if you can believe that one.
So let them show off their fuzzy stuff
while taking a walk or perhaps a run.

August ❶❹
(Day 227 of 366)

Let's see what the Bible📖 has to say:

✝ **Proverbs 12:10** A righteous man cares for the needs of his animal, but the kindest acts of the wicked are cruel.

Lanore is four years old
and loves to smile.
Without even knowing it,
others react for at least a little while.
Try smiling as much as you can,
but it will take some practice.
You use less muscles than frowning
and will feel lighter, just like a kiss.
If you have a neutral face,
your chances are so-so for a frown.
A frown takes two big steps up to a smile,
but a smile is two flights up from feeling down.

August ❶❺

(Day 228 of 366)

Let's see what the Bible📖 has to say:

✝ Proverbs 15:13 A happy heart makes the face cheerful, but heartache crushes the spirit.

Buddy asked a friend if he knows Jesus.
His friend says he *thinks* that he does.
This triggered him to ask a few more questions
and asked him to say a prayer, just because.
His friend trusted Buddy
and asked Jesus to come into his heart.
He also asked for forgiveness of his sins,
so his Lord and Savior will never part.
Buddy hopes that you have taken this step
so you are saved and born again,
because no one knows the day nor hour
that Christ returns, not even *one* knows when.

August ❶⑥

(Day 229 of 366)

Let's see what the Bible📖 has to say:

✝ Mark 13:32 "No one knows about the day or hour, not even the angels in Heaven, nor the Son, but only the Father."

**Lanore went swimming with her Aunt Jules,
which was more like keeping afloat then swimming.
They looked under water and saw a coral reef
and it appeared that it could use a good trimming.
Jules heard the oldest reef was under 5,000 years old,
which fits perfectly with the Bible's account.
It probably formed after the Flood –
millions of years old, would mean a higher amount.**

_～～～～_

August ❶❼
(Day 230 of 366)

Let's see what the Bible📖 has to say:

[†] Ezekiel 47:2 He then brought me out through the north gate and led me around the outside of the outer gate facing east, and the water was flowing from the south side.

Chew-Chew is only three and is the middle child,
which makes him a little on *this* side of wild.
He overheard his mommy's Bible study
when he was playing with toys and his buddy.
They learned about the ten plagues of Egypt
and the glasses of juice they were holding tipped.
They talked about blood, frogs and lice,
which didn't sound very nice.
Then it was flies, boils and pestilence –
hopefully they are all in the past tense.
Hail, locusts and darkness...
that *could* be quite a mess.
To top it off, was death of the first born –
that would have been a lot to mourn.
When Jules' study was complete
and all the ladies put shoes back on their feet.
Chew-Chew held the door opened wide
and hung his head while his Buddy sighed.

✗ 1, 2, 3, 4, 5, 6, 7, 8, 9, 10 ✗

August ❶❽
(Day 231 of 366)

Let's see what the Bible📖 has to say:

✝ Exodus 11:1 Now the Lord had said to Moses, "I will bring one more plague on Pharaoh and on Egypt. After that, he will let you go from here, and when he does, he will drive you out completely."

Bees are scary, bees go buzz,
bees are yellow and some come with fuzz.
Lanore tried to catch one once
and her sister considered her a big dunce.
Then baby sister spread honey on peanut butter,
which made the older one's heart go aflutter.
What's the difference between a wasp and a bee?
A bee is much easier to rhyme with, you see.
When at a picnic lunch with your loved one,
before taking a bite, better check your hotdog bun.
God made some of them to construct a honey comb
that resembles an intricate piece of foam.
If you see one, quicken your step to a hasten –
it may keep you out of a *very* sticky situation.

Buzzzz

August ❶❾
(Day 232 of 366)

Let's see what the Bible📖 has to say:

✝ Proverbs 16:24 Pleasant words are like a honeycomb, sweet to the soul and healing to the bones.

What killed the dinosaurs?
D.J. says it was the Flood.
You may not believe it,
but it runs through *his* blood.
God created the creatures,
along with the other animals,
so when the water came along,
they died with the cows and the bulls.

≈≈≈≈≈≈≈

August 20

(Day 233 of 366)

Let's see what the Bible📖 has to say:

† Genesis 1:24 And God said, "Let the land produce living creatures according to their kinds: livestock, creatures that move along the ground, and wild animals, each according to its kind." And it was so.

Baby No-No turned on the television
to watch her favorite cartoon.
All of a sudden it was interrupted
by a woman whose first name was June.
She said that she has breaking news –
Noah's ark was found in Turkey!
Baby No-No was quite upset
'cause she wanted *stuffing* with *her* gravy.

August ❷❶

(Day 234 of 366)

Let's see what the Bible📖 has to say:

† Genesis 8:4 And on the seventeenth day of the seventh month the ark came to rest on the mountains of Ararat.

Mary Lu was shucking corn
like a good girl from Iowa should do.
All of a sudden she broke out into a sweat
when the temperature was only seventy-two.
Humidity can be an ugly thing
that creeps up on you (or down.)
Just make sure to drink plenty of fluids
and avoid applying makeup like a clown.

August ❷❷

(Day 235 of 366)

Let's see what the Bible📖 has to say:

† Genesis 3:19 "By the sweat of your brow you will eat your food until you return to the ground, since from it you were taken; for dust you are and to dust you will return."

Prince Roderick turned to his Bible
to learn how to be saved.
He already was,
but wanted to share his faith with his friend.
The Book of John says
whoever believes in the Son
will have eternal life.
Jesus will take a broken sole and mend.

August ②③

(Day 236 of 366)

Let's see what the Bible📖 has to say:

✝ John 3:16 "For God so loved the world that He gave His one and only Son, that whoever believes in Him shall not perish but have eternal life."

Kimberella pretty much hates bats
and she knows that's not a nice thing to say,
but when she tries to unlock the door,
they will swoop down and get in her way.
Why must a rat-like mouse have wings to fly
and use a high-frequency yell to help him at night?
"Because God made them that way," is the answer,
"now be quiet, go to bed and shut off the light!"
Mrs. Buckskin dreamt that she was camping
and all the bats had disappeared,
so when she went to kiss her husband,
instead of whiskers, mosquitos hung as his beard.
She awoke and decided that bats are a necessity
to keep the bug population to a minimum,
which brings up another question (oh, brother!)
"Why are there so many bugs...not just have *some*?"

♥ ♥ ♥

August ②④
(Day 237 of 366)

Let's see what the Bible has to say:

† Leviticus 11:19 The stork, any kind of heron, the hoopoe and the bat.

Izzy Ann took a spin
in the wagon her grandpa pulled.
The wheels squeaked as they turned,
because they needed some grease.
Prince Roderick went to his garage
to grab a can of goop.
He applied the stuff to them
and the awful noise did cease.
It reminded Mr. Buckskin
of an article he read last week
about chariot wheels found
on the bottom of the Red Sea.
It proves that God parted the water
for Moses to cross over,
along with the other folks
that he lead to escape death and live free.

≋≋≋≋≋≋≋≋≋≋

❈ ❈ ❈ ❈ ❈ ❈

August ❷❺

(Day 238 of 366)

Let's see what the Bible has to say:

† Exodus 14:25 He made the wheels of their chariots come off so that they had difficulty driving. And the Egyptians said, "Let's get away from the Israelites! The Lord is fighting for them against Egypt."

Sara-Sara stopped at the gas station
on the way to work Monday morning.
She was thinking where oil comes from
as the pump was doing its usual thing.
Most people hear that dinosaurs
are what died and left us the oil,
but humans and all the animals on Earth
also got pressed down below the soil.
So next time you put fuel into your vehicle
and watch the numbers go higher and higher,
think about God's judgment on Earth (the Flood)
and *who* really *is* down under your tire.

Eeeewww!

August ❷❻

(Day 239 of 366)

Let's see what the Bible📖 has to say:

† Genesis 6:17 I am going to bring floodwaters on the earth to destroy all life under the heavens, every creature that has the breath of life in it. Everything on earth will perish.

The Bible talks about water above the firmament,
which Jules knows is another name for the sky.
One theory of what happened during the Flood
is the water vapor barrier came down from on high.
If the barrier was ice, it would have been magnetic,
that would make stars and planets more vivid to gaze at.
The canopy would have protected the earth from the sun
and things would've grown huge and you can count on that.

The Bible speaks of giants
and the fossils were found to prove
that creatures were *huge* in size and stature –
dinosaurs were lizards with more weight to move.

Ø

August ❷❼
(Day 240 of 366)

Let's see what the Bible📖 has to say:

✝ Job 37:18 Can you join him in spreading out the skies, hard as a mirror of cast bronze?

Witty Kitty uses his ears to cross the street
and to get out of the way from pattering little feet.
If he gets mad at Fudgy when he licks his face,
he'll put them back, showing his disgrace.
Ears have been wonderfully designed
by an Almighty God who wants us to hear,
so even if your hearing has faded away,
you can *read* His Word to calm your fear.

👁 👁   👂 👂 🐱

August ❷❽

(Day 241 of 366)

Let's see what the Bible📖 has to say:

✝ Mark 4:23 "If anyone has ears to hear, let him hear."

Auntie K.T. doesn't like fire,
unless it's used to cook a burger,
but if part of a forest burns,
it revitalizes itself as it were.

August ❷❾

(Day 242 of 366)

Let's see what the Bible📖 has to say:

† Jeremiah 17:8 "He will be like a tree planted by the water that sends out its roots by the stream. It does not fear when heat comes; its leaves are always green. It has no worries in a year of drought and never fails to bear fruit."

Does the geologic column even exist?
Buddy says "It sure does!" and he clenches a fist.
He has to bite his tongue whenever he opens a book
to see what science is teaching as he's taking a look.
The only place the column exists is on a page,
because anything but Creation seems to be the rage.
The Flood in Genesis caused the fossils' order, so.....
let's only show columns made of brick and mortar.

August 30
(Day 243 of 366)

Let's see what the Bible has to say:

† James 1:26 If anyone considers himself religious and yet does not keep a tight rein on his tongue, he deceives himself and his religion is worthless.

**Prince Roderick read there was a Thunderbird
that was shot in Eighteen Hundred and Eighty-Two.
He believes that this would be a Pterosaur –
look it up sometime when you need something to do.**

Myth?

August ❸❶

(Day 244 of 366)

Let's see what the Bible📖 has to say:

✝ Matthew 6:26 Look at the birds of the air; they do not sow or reap or store away in barns, and yet your heavenly Father feeds them. Are you not much more valuable than they?

The Buckskin clan loves to go on vacations
and chose science museums as their destinations.
The first one they visited believed in Evolution,
which to this family of believers is equal to pollution.
They still learned a lot about science that was good,
like the composition of metals, rocks and even food.
They thanked the curator and skipped out the door,
knowing that tomorrow they will learn even more.

September ❶
(Day 245 of 366)

Let's see what the Bible📖 has to say:

✝ Proverbs 14:15 A simple man believes anything, but a prudent man gives thoughts to his steps.

The Buckskin clan climbed back into their car
and drove to the Creation museum that wasn't far.
They learned about how God designed everything:
people, animals, plants, snow and rain.
The curator at this interesting and wonderful place
said they could find foot prints of the human race
down in a river bed that isn't very far away.
They skipped out the door to see them the same day.

September ❷
(Day 246 of 366)

Let's see what the Bible📖 has to say:

✝ Colossians 1:16 For by Him all things were created: things in Heaven and on earth, visible and invisible, whether thrones or powers or rulers or authorities; all things were created by Him and for Him.

The Buckskin clan arrived at the Paluxy River
and stayed until the moon shone as a little sliver.
They found some dino footprints and humans' as well
next to each other, just before Fudgy slipped and fell.
They're not as prominent as when first discovered,
because they are eroding away, they all had heard.
Some scientist who didn't want to believe the facts,
said that a dino with human feet made the tracks!
If *you* don't want to believe, you *have* that right,
but it's hard to deny something within your eyesight.

⊙ ⊙

September ❸
(Day 247 of 366)

Let's see what the Bible has to say:

☨ John 7:38 "Whoever believes in me, as the Scripture has said, streams of living water will flow from within himself."

Jack ran over to his father's garage...
actually, he drove his truck, since he's not a fool.
He wanted to see if Prince Roderick could help him
find a way to fix his truck with the perfect tool.
Mr. Buckskin handed him one and dug deeper,
Jack looked it over, thinking about back in the day.
People generations ago, when the Bible was written,
would make a tool first before they made headway.
They would need a hammer and hatchet,
so they could pound things out or split them in two.
A straight-edge and plumb-line would also be needed
to make things fall in place, which is smart to do.
An awl or engraver was used for holes and etching
to puncture leather for clothing and labeling things.
A knife and chisel would be for cutting or shaping,
but never, not *ever* be used to loosen rings!
Jack's dad finally found what he was looking for,
but the sun had set and his son's truck was long gone.
He decided to give his own vehicle a once over
and Kimberella didn't see him until it was dawn.

September ❹
(Day 248 of 366)

Let's see what the Bible📖 has to say:

✝ Jeremiah 23:29 "Is not any word like fire," declares the Lord, "and like a hammer that breaks a rock into pieces?"

**Kimberella has a simple way
to believe in millions of years.
You just have to shut your eyes
and use your imagination.
In fact, it's as easy as A, B, C
(if you will pardon the cliché.)
A man from a monkey takes
<u>A</u>nything <u>B</u>ut <u>C</u>reation!**

😐

September ❺

(Day 249 of 366)

Let's see what the Bible📖 has to say:

✝ Isaiah 6:10 "Make the heart of this people calloused; make their ears dull and close their eyes. Otherwise they might see with their eyes, hear with their ears, understand with their hearts, and turn and be healed."

Witty Kitty climbed a tree
and opened a book to read.
He wanted to find out the age
of the oldest living tree.
Five Thousand Sixty-Two
was the answer that he found.
The cat *about* fell off his branch,
but his claws let him be.
"That makes perfect sense!"
he muttered to himself,
"It probably sprung up
after the great Flood."
When he sits on a ledge
of the science room's window,
talk of billions of years
really boils his blood.

September ❻

(Day 250 of 366)

Let's see what the Bible📖 has to say:

✝ Ecclesiastes 11:3 If clouds are full of water, they pour rain upon the earth. Whether a tree falls to the south or to the north, in the place where it falls, there will it lie.

Sometimes a person will tell Rochelle
that they think the Bible contradicts itself.
She believes this is the reason why
God's holy Word collects dust on their shelf.
They get confused about when things were created,
because some things get mentioned again later on.
It's because the Garden of Eden was being formed
to name the animals and so kiss *that* theory gone.

September ❼

(Day 251 of 366)

Let's see what the Bible📖 has to say:

† Genesis 2:8 Now the Lord God had planted a garden in the east, in Eden; and there He put the man He had formed.

Today when Fudgy read his Bible,
it talked about wisdom.
On the way out to the kitchen,
he stubbed his big toe.
He wanted to sneak a cookie,
but he decided not to be naughty.
He used his wisdom to stay out of trouble,
like a man (or doggy) in the know.

Just say no! "Woof!"

September ❽
(Day 252 of 366)

Let's see what the Bible📖 has to say:

† Proverbs 10:23 A fool finds pleasure in evil conduct, a man of understanding delights in wisdom.

Jules took her kiddies to the museum
and saw a skeleton of a male elephant.
She thought it strange that the trunk wasn't there,
since it's the most recognized part of the gent.
She told her brood that the trunk has fingers –
one or two, depending on the species
and up to forty thousand muscles that can lift
seven hundred seventy pounds like a breeze.
It can smell four times better
than an ordinary old blood hound.
It can be used to snorkel while crossing a riverbed,
instead of taking the long way around on ground.
Chew-Chew and Izzy Ann agreed with their mother
that the skeleton *should* show the great trunk,
but then again if it did...
no bones about it, it would be a bunch of bunk!

September ❾

(Day 253 of 366)

Let's see what the Bible📖 has to say:

† Proverbs 14:30 A heart at peace gives life to the body, but envy rots the bones.

The more Prince Roderick listens to his audio tapes of the Bible read by a man (not the author)... the more he finds out how much God doesn't favor a fool who lacks wisdom *and* much more.

September ❶❶

(Day 254 of 366)

Let's see what the Bible has to say:

† Proverbs 29:9 If a wise man goes to court with a fool, the fool rages and scoffs, and there is no peace.

If D.J. were aboard Noah's ark,
he would have studied the night hawk.
A night owl would be more appropriate,
but rhyming the word "owl" makes Kimberella balk.
The night hawk is a nocturnal bird (duh)
and has long wings, short legs and a bill.
Instead of trees, they nest on the ground –
they eat insects, so every ant *better* stay *in* the hill.

≈≈≈⌂≈≈≈

September ❶❶

(Day 255 of 366)

Let's see what the Bible📖 has to say:

✝ Isaiah 34:14 Desert creatures will meet with hyenas, and wild goats will bleat to each other; there the night creatures will also repose and find themselves places of rest.

Izzy Ann learned what Jesus did for us on the cross
in Sunday School, the week before last.
God's son was born in a manger
and quite a few years have passed.
He performed miracles, doing God's will
and then died on the cross for our sins.
On the third day He rose to prove to all that
He will come back and whoever is saved...wins!

September ❶❷

(Day 256 of 366)

Let's see what the Bible📖 has to say:

✝ **1** Corinthians 1:18 For the message of the cross is foolishness to those who are perishing, but to us who are saved it is the power of God.

Jack and Sara-Sara turned to the Bible
to learn about marriage.
This was when they were dating
to see if they could mesh.
The Book of Genesis said that a man
leaves his father and mother
to cling to his wife,
so the two of them become one flesh.

† 📖

🧍 + 🧍 = ♥

September ❶❸
(Day 257 of 366)

Let's see what the Bible📖 has to say:

† Genesis 2:24 For this reason a man will leave his father and mother and be united to his wife, and they will become one flesh.

Auntie K.T. was climbing a ladder
to change a light bulb in her bat house.
Why would you need a light in there?
So you can scream while seeing a mouse?
Kimberella doesn't like bats
and has told Auntie this more than just once.
Whether a rodent has wings or not,
she becomes something of a dunce.
Mrs. Buckskin *supposes* that they have a place,
because this world would be overrun by bugs,
but she wishes that God would have designed them
with kitten faces, instead of ratty looking mugs.

September ❶❹

(Day 258 of 366)

Let's see what the Bible📖 has to say:

✝ Isaiah 41:10 So do not fear, for I am with you; do not be dismayed, for I am your God. I will strengthen you and help; I will uphold you with my righteous right hand.

Lanore was learning how to ride a bike
and fell off the seat and onto her tail bone.
The pain reminded her about the time
her leg was stuck inside of a trombone.
Why do we have a tailbone, if one is not needed?
Is it from back when we were a monkey?
We were NEVER a monkey, so that's not the answer!
It's the end of the spine for you and for me.

September ❶❺

(Day 259 of 366)

Let's see what the Bible📖 has to say:

✝ **Genesis 2:7 The Lord God formed the man from the dust of the ground and breathed into his nostrils the breath of life, and the man became a living being.**

Buddy went fishing down by the lake,
which was a great place to throw in his poles.
He could see right through the very clean water
with eyes that are much keener than a mole's.
As he waited for something to bite on his bait,
he pondered about fossils forming fast.
If a bunch of fish were buried quickly
and sediment by the tons hardened like a cast,
then fossils didn't have to take millions of years
like some of the text books say.
They could have formed during a catastrophic flood
to many scientists' and scoffers' dismay.

~~~~~~~~

September ❶❻

(Day 260 of 366)

Let's see what the Bible has to say:

⊺ **Genesis 6:17** I am going to bring floodwaters on the earth to destroy all life under the heavens, every creature that has the breath of life in it. Everything on earth will perish.

**Kimberella looked up her name
to see what the computer said.
"A 600 million year old fossil,"
is what Mrs. Buckskin had read.
"That's a laugh!" she thought to herself,
"I'm not that old, at least not yet!"
She also knows something else that is true:
The *Earth* isn't either, on *that* you can bet.**

September ❶❼

(Day 261 of 366)

Let's see what the Bible📖 has to say:

✝ Psalm 71:9 Do not cast me away when I am old; do not forsake me when my strength is gone.

**Baby No-No don't know nothin',
but she *does* know when she's hungry.
The body tells us what we are craving –
if we need salt, sugar or a veggie.**

⚫⚫⚫ = *Gurgle*

September ❶❽

(Day 262 of 366)

Let's see what the Bible📖 has to say:

✝ Matthew 5:6 Blessed are those who hunger and thirst for righteousness, for they will be filled.

Jules went to the newsstand to buy the daily news.
She walked into the living room humming to the blues.
After only two minutes, she put the paper down.
Her husband, The General, couldn't believe her frown.
"What's the matter, dear?" he said with great concern.
"I only read the *good* news...when will I *ever* learn?"
"We can line the bird's cage," he said, then he laughed.
The bird said, "If they think *I'll*
read it, they're *both* daft!"

September ❶❾

(Day 263 of 366)

Let's see what the Bible📖 has to say:

† Psalm 112:7 He will have no fear of bad news; his heart is steadfast, trusting in the Lord.

Sometimes Fudgy feels very sick
when he gets a midnight snack from the garbage.
For the *rest* of us human beings,
our bodies can let us know what to avoid in the fridge.
We suffer from nausea, headaches and bloating.
God designed us perfectly, He knew what He was doing.
Listen to yourself and God when feeling kind of funny,
and also you should avoid things that you are chewing.

🐕

September 20

(Day 264 of 366)

Let's see what the Bible📖 has to say:

✝ **1 Corinthians 11:29** For anyone who eats and drinks without recognizing the body of the Lord eats and drinks judgement on himself.

Mary Lu studied in school
about some pyramids found in Egypt.
She said they look like four triangles
leaning together as if they are tipped.
Mary Lu learned there are one hundred eighteen
of the monuments built for a tomb.
That's quite a few people who are buried
way down inside of a stone-like womb.

△▲△▲△▲

September ❷❶
(Day 265 of 366)

Let's see what the Bible📖 has to say:

✝ Matthew 7:13 "Enter through the narrow gate. For wide is the gate and broad is the road that leads to destruction, and many enter through it."

Kimberella likes to go to museums
to see rocks and an animal's track,
but one thing she finds kind of amusing
is when they say billions of years as a fact.
The great Flood in Noah's day
made the Grand Canyon in a hurry.
A statement like that makes some scientists
throw their hats in the ring with fury.
If they could just put aside
the age of the earth as billions,
they could see that a flood *can* prove
a few of Earth's features times millions.

September ❷❷
(Day 266 of 366)

Let's see what the Bible📖 has to say:

✝ Proverbs 14:29 A patient man has great understanding, but a quick-tempered man displays folly.

**Chew-Chew was listening to a Bible story
about Leviathan, the fire-breathing dragon.
When he gets taken to the park by Grandpa,
he pretends to see them while in his wagon.
"Dinosaur" wasn't a word when the Bible was written...
they called them dragons and some breathed fire.
They lived at the same time as humans did –
created by God who resides somewhere up higher.**

September ❷❸

(Day 267 of 366)

Let's see what the Bible📖 has to say:

✝ **Psalm 18:8** Smoke rose from his nostrils; consuming fire came from his mouth.

Witty Kitty wanted his lunch,
so he arched his back into a hunch.
Then the cat jumped up on the countertop,
knocking over a can of root beer soda pop.
Kimberella shouted, "Didn't it ever occur to you
to use a step stool or wear a taller shoe?"
The feline just shook his head at Mrs. Buckskin
thinking, *"Please step aside so I can open my tin."*
Sometimes we should *all* stop and think
while we're washing the dishes at the sink:
"Nothing occurs to God Almighty –
all knowing...all powerful...all is He!"

Oh, yeah!

September ❷❹

(Day 268 of 366)

Let's see what the Bible📖 has to say:

† Matthew 24:36 "No one knows about that day or hour, not even the angels in Heaven, nor the Son, but only the Father."

Sara-Sara knows
that each child is unique -
which ones will hoot and holler
and the ones who will only squeak.
Some kids will run
when they hear the bell ring.
Others will walk slower
than raccoons in the spring.
In the lunch room a child
may beg for an extra treat,
while his neighbor at the table
will nibble on a cracker of wheat.
We all have unique DNA
that is especially made for one and all –
the Economic teacher went to the thrift store
and Sara-Sara headed for the mall.

September ❷❺

(Day 269 of 366)

Let's see what the Bible📖 has to say:

[†] Isaiah 43:7 "Everyone who is called by my name, whom I created for my glory, whom I formed and made."

**Mary Lu was admiring her new baby cousin
and Baby No-No don't know nothin' –
but, Mary Lu *knows* that Jesus was born a baby,
and He didn't stay that way, not even maybe.
Jesus is God in the flesh, who came down to save,
because of our sins, it is His life that He gave.
So even though babies are precious and cute,
it's only for a little while, to this you cannot dispute.
God could have had Jesus appear on Earth as a man,
but He chose to make Him like us, *because* God can.**

September ❷❻

(Day 270 of 366)

Let's see what the Bible📖 has to say:

✝ John 1:14 The Word became flesh and made His dwelling among us. We have seen His glory of the One and Only, who came from the Father, full of grace and truth.

Lanore turned to her Bible
to learn about relationships,
because in preschool she didn't like
a girl at her table.
The Book of Philippians said to treat others
better than yourself,
so she took her favorite sucker
and gave it to her newfound friend, Mabel.

September ❷❼

(Day 271 of 366)

Let's see what the Bible📖 has to say:

☨ Philippians 2:3 Do nothing out of selfish ambition or vain conceit, but in humility consider others better than yourselves.

**D.J. was buttoning up his shirt
to play at a dance after his friends wed.
When he couldn't find his cuff links,
he used a couple of clothespins instead.
When he looked in the mirror before he took off,
it reminded him of a discussion of late.
The so-called missing links that were found
are *still* missing as of today's date.
Humans were formed as humans
in the beginning, just as God had said.
In His holy Bible that He had written,
we all can put *this* subject to bed.**

September ❷❽

(Day 272 of 366)

Let's see what the Bible📖 has to say:

✝ **1** Corinthians 15:45 So it is written: "The first man Adam became a living being," the last Adam, a life-giving spirit.

Not that long ago,
most people believed in a young earth.
In fact, they probably didn't even have
to think of such a thing.
The Bible was read aloud in homes
with the family members gathered around.
They worshipped their God
and more than likely someone would sing.
Praises to God, the Creator
and Designer of all were given.
In the beginning means just that
in the Book of Genesis.
Now a person is considered ignorant
if they go against Evolution.
One time that Prince Roderick is willing
to be called "ignorant" is this.

September ②⑨

(Day 273 of 366)

Let's see what the Bible📖 has to say:

✝ **1** Peter 4:16 However, if you suffer as a Christian, do not be ashamed, but praise God that you bear that name.

Izzy Ann was running very fast
to catch up with the ice cream truck.
She ordered an ice cream cone with nuts on top
and handed over to the driver one measly buck.
"That's not enough!" the gentleman scolded the child,
"That won't even pay for the air in my tire."
"My daddy always tells me that the air is free,"
But, she rolled two quarters to him straight as a wire.
The oxygen we breathe *is* provided to us without cost.
It's a gift from God that He made sure was available.
Just like all of the plants and trees He created,
to give us vegetables and fruit to eat at our table.

Free!

September 30

(Day 274 of 366)

Let's see what the Bible📖 has to say:

† Genesis 2:7 The Lord God formed the man from the dust of the ground and breathed into his nostrils the breath of life, and the man became a living being.

The Buckskins know that you need money
for things like food, clothing and a house,
but it's also true that the root of most evil
does come to someone like a greedy louse.
There's a perfect verse about one's finances –
it sums it up if you will pardon the pun.
Try to be content with what you have
and worship God even if you have none.

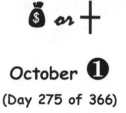

October ❶
(Day 275 of 366)

Let's see what the Bible📖 has to say:

†️ **1** Timothy 6:10 For the love of money is a root of all kinds of evil. Some people, eager for money, have wandered from the faith and pierced themselves with many griefs.

Today when Prince Roderick read his Bible,
it talked about government.
Afterward, he sat by the fireplace
to reflect in his very happy abode.
Kimberella handed him a mug of hot cocoa
and asked what he learned that day.
He said, "To pay taxes, revenue, respect and honor
to those to whom it's owed."

October ❷
(Day 276 of 366)

Let's see what the Bible📖 has to say:

✝ Romans 13:7 Give everyone what you owe him: If you owe taxes, pay taxes; if revenue, then revenue; if respect, then respect; if honor, then honor.

Sara-Sara told her class one day:
"Sometimes cats and dogs
and other animals, too
have a couple of colors of fur
and sometimes quite a few.
If you brush aside their fur
and look at what's underneath,
you may see different colors of skin,
but hopefully only white for teeth."
The children went home amazed
at what they had learned that day.
The next morning Tommy was crying,
because his turtle wasn't made that way.
He said he doesn't own a dog
or even one measly cat.
So, she let him try it on Mr. Jingles,
which happened to be the janitor's pet rat.

October ❸
(Day 277 of 366)

Let's see what the Bible📖 has to say:

† **Proverbs 12:10** A righteous man cares for the needs of his animal, but the kindest acts of the wicked are cruel.

**Izzy Ann turned to her Bible
to learn how to hunt for food.
She watched a video with her daddy
about an archer who shot a doe.
The Book of Genesis tells of a boy
that God kept company with
who grew up, lived in the wild,
and became an expert with a bow.**

October ❹
(Day 278 of 366)

Let's see what the Bible📖 has to say:

✝ Genesis 21:20 God was with the boy as he grew up. He lived in the desert and became an archer.

Prince Roderick went for a walk
down by the creek in the country.
He was reminded of Jesus walking on water
and Moses parting the Red Sea.
Jesus performed many miracles
like giving sight to a blind man.
He also cured a leper of his ills
and mended a withered hand.
A bleeding woman touched his cloak,
because she believed she would be cured.
A man who was paralyzed was able to walk –
maybe the deaf-mute, who was healed, had heard.

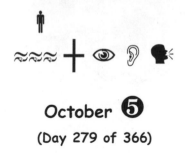

October ❺

(Day 279 of 366)

Let's see what the Bible📖 has to say:

† Matthew 14:25 During the fourth watch of the night Jesus went out to them, walking on the lake.

Fudgy heard his so-called master
reading an article by the light of a candle:
"Monkeys peel bananas from the bottom up...
I wonder if it's so they end up with a handle?"
Kimberella shot back rather quickly,
which isn't a very nice way to be,
"This proves one thing without a shadow of a doubt,
people don't, because they never *were* a monkey!"

🕯 **0%**

October ❻

(Day 280 of 366)

Let's see what the Bible📖 has to say:

✝ Psalm 139:14 I praise you because I am fearfully and wonderfully made; your works are wonderful, I know you full well.

Today when Witty Kitty read his Bible,
it talked about laws.
He climbed down from the shelf
and rubbed against Izzy Ann's dress.
"I've told you how many times
not to do that!" she scolded the cat.
He remembered that practicing sinning,
is practicing lawlessness.

October ❼

(Day 281 of 366)

Let's see what the Bible📖 has to say:

✝ **1** John 3:4 Everyone who sins breaks the law; in fact,
sin is lawlessness.

**Our Lord, Jesus Christ, can heal us of our pain,
whether it is spiritual or physical, so we can be sane.
Whatever ills you may be suffering, be sure to know,
Jules believes He will treat *your* pain just like a foe.**

✝

October ❽

(Day 282 of 366)

Let's see what the Bible has to say:

⌖ Jeremiah 17:14 Heal me, O Lord, and I will be healed;
save me and I will be saved, for you are the One I praise.

Lanore put on her wings
that she keeps under her bed.
She likes to pretend she can fly,
but her legs feel like they are made of lead.
Mary Lu tried to tell her it just won't work
and explained it to her like this:
"Birds have hollow bones to help *them* fly
easier than legs with shoes, little Sis."
Their bones actually weigh less than feathers,
which made Lanore more confused than ever.
"Why isn't the phrase 'as light as a feather,'
really 'as light as a bone?' she prodded her.

October ❾
(Day 283 of 366)

Let's see what the Bible📖 has to say:

✝ Isaiah 40:31 But those who hope in the Lord will renew their strength. They will soar on wings like eagles; they will run and not grow weary, they will walk and not be faint.

Witty Kitty likes to take walks,
but not on a leash by his owner.
Except for his meals served to him,
he could live out his life as a loner.
The cat thinks about nomads who roamed deserts,
walking for miles on end in the scorching hot sand.
They probably went from one continent to another
before the water came down and flooded the land.
The continents are not corks floating in a bathtub,
they are land masses, some with water, some without.
The water covers over the low and we see the high.
Witty Kitty will take a boat and that is *no* doubt.

October ❶⓪

(Day 284 of 366)

Let's see what the Bible📖 has to say:

† Genesis 1:9 And God said, "Let the water under the sky be gathered to one place, and let dry ground appear." And it was so.

If Buddy were aboard Noah's ark,
he would have studied Leviathan,
a fire breathing dragon.
He would come in handy for lighting cigarettes,
but with a wooden boat, there would be none!
The dragon is spoken of in almost every culture –
a hollow chamber in his head would work out just fine.
In Job, the Bible speaks of its neesings,
which from him a light doth shine.

≈≈≈⌂≈≈≈

October ❶❶

(Day 285 of 366)

Let's see what the Bible📖 has to say:

⊤ Job 40:1 "Can you pull in the leviathan with a fishhook or tie down his tongue with a rope?"

Kimberella says the word "behemoth"
in the Bible describes a dinosaur.
Some footnotes say it's either
a hippopotamus or an elephant.
Sure, they both have heavy bones,
but the tail is like a cedar?
Can you see those things looking like a tree?
Mrs. Buckskin sure enough can't.

~ or J

October ①②

(Day 286 of 366)

Let's see what the Bible📖 has to say:

✝ Job 40:17 For God did not endow her with wisdom or give her a share of good sense.

Prince Roderick was looking
at a government form
and it asked if weather was the cause
of an animals' death.
Obviously this question
made him scratch his head thinking,
"What about snuffing out babies
before their first breath?!"
Mr. Buckskin likes animals
and even has one as a pet.
He thinks they want to add
to the myth of global warming.
If a beast was killed by it,
the activists could go wild,
saying that humans are the cause
for all the harming.

October ❶❸

(Day 287 of 366)

Let's see what the Bible📖 has to say:

✝ Nahum 1:3 The Lord is slow to anger and great in power; the Lord will not leave the guilty unpunished. His way is in the whirlwind and the storm, and clouds are the dust of His feet.

D.J. received a G.P.S./Phone for a Christmas present
from a band member who shall remain nameless.
She was tired of him losing his way –
it was Kimberella, she must confess.
D.J. went out of town for a wedding gig
and the device told him to prepare to park and walk.
Also, he should swing by the store for some tennies –
he liked it when phones weren't programmed to talk.

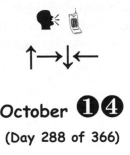

October ①④

(Day 288 of 366)

Let's see what the Bible📖 has to say:

⟨†⟩ **Deuteronomy 22:4** If you see your brother's donkey or his ox fallen on the road, do not ignore it. Help him get it to its feet.

Izzy Ann likes to put on angels wings
and "fly" around her living room.
Chew-Chew will watch her flit about
as their mommy sweeps around with a broom.
The Bible speaks of oodles of angels
to help us living beings out on this globe.
They will guide and watch over us
and if need be, lead us by grabbing a lobe.

October ❶❺

(Day 289 of 366)

Let's see what the Bible📖 has to say:

✝ Hebrews 1:14 Are not angels ministering spirits sent to serve those who will inherit salvation?

**Kimberella went to the doctor
for a bad case of hiccups she acquired one night.
They seemed to magically disappear
as she was scared by the report she was losing height.
She shrunk in size by one and a half inches,
somewhere from last June or July.
She asked Rochelle the next day at work,
"Why couldn't I have lost them around my thigh?"**

October ❶❻

(Day 290 of 366)

Let's see what the Bible📖 has to say:

✝ Isaiah 41:10 So do not fear, for I am with you; do not be dismayed, for I am your God. I will strengthen you and help you; I will uphold you with my righteous right hand.

**Sara-Sara and Jack were having a discussion
whether or not the Bible is poetic.
They searched on the internet for quite a while,
after dealing with dial-up, they both felt a little sick.
The husband and wife decided to do what was best
and took turns reading God's holy Word aloud,
that way they could find out the old fashioned way –
it would've made their pastor very proud.
There is a lot of information on the Bible and poetry
and you may want to check it out someday soon.
Go ahead and look it up on *your* computer today,
then read God's Book while eating lunch at noon.
What *does* rhyme with poetic?**

October ❶❼

(Day 291 of 366)

Let's see what the Bible has to say:

🕆 **1** Corinthians 13:1 If I speak in tongues of men and of angels, but have not love, I am only a resounding gong or a clanging cymbal.

Mary Lu was riding the waves on her boogie board
in the Atlantic Ocean in the middle of October.
This should *only* be attempted while fully awake –
with the water that cold, she was able to stay sober.
She fantasized about swimming under the water
about two to three miles down
to see a whole other world beneath the water,
including a section that would resemble her town.
She laid on her board and dreamt of mountains,
valleys, cliffs, hills and plateaus.
Two worlds in one is pretty amazing –
How can it all exist? God surely knows!

October ❶❽

(Day 292 of 366)

Let's see what the Bible📖 has to say:

✝ Job 38:16 "Have you journeyed to the springs of the sea or walked in the recesses of the deep?"

Jules turned to her Bible,
to learn how to care for animals,
because her kids wanted a pet,
she heard in a song that they sung.
The Book of James told her
that all kinds of creatures are being tamed –
done by mankind...however,
no human can seem to tame the tongue.

October ❶❾

(Day 293 of 366)

Let's see what the Bible📖 has to say:

✝ James 3:7 All kinds of animals, birds, reptiles and creatures of the sea are being tamed and have been tamed by man.

Prince Roderick, Buddy and D.J.
went to a sportsmen's outdoor picnic.
Having a picnic indoors would be silly,
but then again, there *wouldn't* have been a tick.
D.J. got bitten by one of the rascals
and a red target pattern soon appeared.
Luckily, he didn't get the Lyme disease,
however, he received the doctor bill that he feared.
Just one little bug can bring a big person down,
just like a little sin can turn into a bad habit.
After you've been outside, check yourself over
and then study God's Word and pray as you sit.

☹ ✝ ☺

October ❷⓪
(Day 294 of 366)

Let's see what the Bible📖 has to say:

✝ John 3:4 "How can a man be born when he is old?" Nicodemus asked, "Surely he cannot enter a second time into his mother's womb to be born!"

Auntie K.T. went to Eureka Springs, Arkansas
to check out the Ozarks and do some hiking.
Then she saw upon a sign about a Holy Land tour
while she was getting some needed exercise, biking.
They had the woman by the well telling her story,
Moses also gave a detailed speech of his life.
Then off to the manger where Baby Jesus was born;
you can also hear the story of Lot and his wife.
On and off the bus to a cave for the Last Supper –
there was so much more for her to see and hear
at this replica of the Holy Land in Arkansas.
It's located by the Passion Play, that she holds dear.

October ❷❶

(Day 295 of 366)

Let's see what the Bible📖 has to say:

✝ **1 Peter 2:21** To this you were called, because Christ suffered for you, leaving you an example, that you should follow His steps.

Earthquakes are very scary...
even Chew-Chew who's only three knows that.
One could turn Witty Kitty
into a *very* nervous cat.
You don't have to live in California
to have one tremble under your feet.
You could be in Iowa driving your car
and have it feel like rocks are in the street.
The Tribulation is coming
as the Bible clearly states.
There will be earthquakes so large,
that people will be cancelling all of their dates.

October ❷❷
(Day 296 of 366)

Let's see what the Bible📖 has to say:

† Revelation 11:13 At that very hour there was a severe earthquake and a tenth of the city collapsed. Seven thousand people were killed in the earthquake, and the survivors were terrified and gave glory to the God of Heaven.

**One of Kimberella's statements is as follows:
"I'm always in trouble or so it appears."
If she does or doesn't do something,
the fault lies with her...here comes the tears.
She tries not to sound paranoid
and doesn't want to say she's busier than most,
but whenever something goes wrong,
the blame lays on her, like peanut butter upon toast.**

October ❷❸

(Day 297 of 366)

Let's see what the Bible📖 has to say:

† Psalm 34:6 This poor man called, and the Lord heard him; He saved him out of all his troubles.

Rabbits, rabbits everywhere –
not only in your neighborhood,
but also in the country, across the nation
and other continents, as they should.
They are an example of micro Evolution
where small changes just make sense.
Like the ability to have differing fur
such as color, whether thin or dense.
Buddy saw one in Alaska that was white
and its fur thicker than his mustache,
but when he visited Florida last year,
it was brown and thinner like his cash.
Micro Evolution is acceptable
and can be proven over and over again,
but Macro is a whole other story...
the bunny would have to grow a fin.

October ❷❹

(Day 298 of 366)

Let's see what the Bible📖 has to say:

✝ Leviticus 11:6 The rabbit; though it chews the cud; does not have a split hoof; it is unclean for you.

Prince Roderick likes to go hunting,
but he only hunts what he is willing to eat.
The Bible mentions weapons quite often,
which are used to defend and flat out defeat.
There is the sword, the knife and ordinary weapons
that are listed throughout God's Word.
They are used for big and small battles between men,
not to supply the Thanksgiving table with a big bird.

October ❷❺

(Day 299 of 366)

Let's see what the Bible📖 has to say:

† Isaiah 2:4 He will judge between the nations and will settle disputes for many peoples. They will beat their swords into plowshares and their spears into pruning hooks. Nation will not take up sword against nation; nor will they train for war anymore.

The General wants to know what is the "matter"
that the Big Bang folks say is what got together.
Did it all decide at once to form and then shrink,
then spin around and around like a ball on a tether?

October ❷❻

(Day 300 of 366)

Let's see what the Bible📖 has to say:

✝ **Hebrews 11:3** By faith we understand that the universe was formed at God's command, so that what is seen was not made out of what was visible.

Jules went on a trip to Egypt to find out for herself
if the Great Pyramid of Giza was built out of rocks.
She packed a suitcase with her detective kit in it
and threw in a sun visor, shades and camel clad socks.
Jules climbed the Pyramid, praying she wouldn't fall.
She read that something was to be placed up on its top,
but all she saw was a few birds flying around her head.
She decided to sit down and have
pretzels and a soda pop.
On her way back down the side, she peered into a hole.
She saw a long narrow shaft that went upward to the sky,
at the bottom of the monument, she looked into another
and saw that is was wider and going down...oh, my!
This is *one* of the correlations to the Bible's teaching,
that the path to Heaven is a narrow and upward battle
and the way to the pit is wide and downward,
which many choose to travel on like a herd of cattle.
After hours and days of taking down notes,
she wrote on the last page of her journal once and for all:
"Maybe the other pyramids were to honor a man's life,
but the Pyramid of Giza is for God",
and put on her shawl.

▲▲▲ △

October ❷❼

(Day 301 of 366)

Let's see what the Bible📖 has to say:

† Isaiah 19:19 In that day there will be an altar to the
Lord in the heart of Egypt, and a monument to the Lord at
its border.

D.J. turned to his Bible
to learn about sacrifice.
He wants to grow as a Christian
and do what he should.
The Book of Hebrews said sacrifices
that are pleasing to God,
is sharing what you *have*
and *not* to neglect doing good.

October ❷❽

(Day 302 of 366)

Let's see what the Bible has to say:

⟊ Hebrews 13:16 And do not forget to do good and to share with others, for with such sacrifices God is pleased.

Lanore had a visitor come to her school
to have her class give a fingerprint sample.
The policeman said they keep the records on file,
as he stepped aside not to succumb to a trample.
Lanore and her classmates were anxious to see
how their fingers would look covered in blue.
He had them roll each finger and thumb
onto a paper held down by his assistant, Sue.
The teacher said how amazing it is
that we each were given our personal identity;
like snowflakes falling from the sky,
there always seems to be more than plenty.

October ❷❾

(Day 303 of 366)

Let's see what the Bible📖 has to say:

† Galatians 3:28 There is neither Jew nor Greek, slave nor free, male nor female, for you are all one in Christ Jesus.

Chew-Chew just cut in a new tooth.
That's good for him to chew his food.
If he had to gum it until he was an adult,
he would grow up to be a very scrawny dude.
A shark can have thousands of teeth in a lifetime
to eat scrawny boys if they're not being careful,
so please take good care of your choppers...
carry a file while surfing to make sharp fangs dull.

VVVVVV
∧ ∧ ∧ ∧ ∧ ∧

October ❸⓪
(Day 304 of 366)

Let's see what the Bible has to say:

⊹ Galatians 5:15 If you keep on biting and devouring each other, watch out or you will be destroyed by each other.

When Jack was a little boy,
going to the moon sounded like fun.
He said he wanted to be an astronaut
and take a rocket on a trial run.
He found out in school that real spacemen
found little cosmic dust on the moon,
which surprised them immensely
and almost caused them to swoon.
It was taught that the universe is older than dirt
and the dust would be thicker times oodles,
but the amount that was found that day
made them say to that theory, "Toodles!"

⊱— ☾

October ❸❶

(Day 305 of 366)

Let's see what the Bible📖 has to say:

⊺ Genesis 3:19 "By the sweat of your brow you will eat your food until you return to the ground, since from it you were taken; for dust you are and to dust you will return."

Today when Sara-Sara read her Bible,
it talked about faith.
And with it, God by grace,
will save you from being toast.
Just remember that it is not
from doing your good works –
it is a gift from God,
so that no one may boast.

November ❶

(Day 306 of 366)

Let's see what the Bible📖 has to say:

✝ Ephesians 2:8-9 For it is by grace you have been saved, through faith – and this not from yourselves, it is the gift of God – not by works, so that no one can boast.

Fudgy took a trip to Grand Canyon
on a field trip riddled with rules.
The bus driver told the furry beast
that he better not talk to the mules.
Fudgy, being the rebel that he is,
hopped on the head mule's back.
As they were going down to the abyss,
he opened his jaws and started to yack.
Fudgy asked his friend who was underneath,
"Do you think the river did this much damage?"
The beast of burden shook his head saying,
"The Flood," that's all he could manage.
"When tons of water flows very quickly
through soft sediment and such,
the result is canyons and valleys."
Fudgy heard as he scarfed down his lunch.
When the trip up the hill had ended
and the pooch got back onto the bus,
he figured out that the driver was brainwashed,
which explained all the fuss.
He didn't want Fudgy to be talking
to an animal who's wiser than he,
because since the doggy can't keep his mouth shut,
he'll be spreading the word and won't let it be.

🐕 *Blah, blah, blah....*

November ❷

(Day 307 of 366)

Let's see what the Bible📖 has to say:

✝ **Numbers 22:28** Then the Lord opened the donkey's mouth, and she said to Balaam, "What have I done to you to make you beat me these three times?"

Sara-Sara was teaching her classroom of children the difference between Creation and Evolution. She tried really hard not to laugh out loud when reading the Big Bang theory as a solution. The mere thought of matter getting together and squeezing itself smaller than a period on a page, to Sara-Sara is just plain ridiculous when an exclamation point would be the rage!

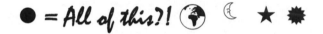

November ❸
(Day 308 of 366)

Let's see what the Bible📖 has to say:

✝ Isaiah 45:12 It is I who made the earth and created mankind upon it. My own hands stretched out the heavens; I marshaled their starry hosts.

**Kimberella brings cookies to the Chocolate Factory,
without caring if everyone likes them or not.
She will bring them if just *one* person
will have their day brightened on the spot.
Nobody else has to return the favor,
they can eat them or just walk away –
they can choose to ignore the gesture...
it's about giving freely each and every day.**

November ❹

(Day 309 of 366)

Let's see what the Bible📖 has to say:

† **2 Corinthians 5:15** And He died for all, that those who live should no longer live for themselves but for Him who died for them and was raised again.

Baby No-No may not know nothin',
but sleeping is her cup of tea.
She can do it for long stretches of time
that would be unheard of for you and me.
She doesn't realize that she grows in her sleep
and that it helps a baby get the energy they need
to cry really loud in the morning
and throw food on the floor as they feed.
Rest for adults is just as important,
because God designed our bodies to sleep.
You need the rest to run like a top,
so shut your eyes and breathe in deep.

November ❺

(Day 310 of 366)

Let's see what the Bible📖 has to say:

✝ Psalm 127:2 In vain you rise early and stay up late, toiling for food to eat – for He grants sleep to those He loves.

Mary Lu does not like bugs,
or at least when she was two.
It would scare her so when a spider
creeped his way to her shoe.
To her Grandmother Buckskin,
a tick is much worse,
because they hide in her hair,
which can make her a tad bit terse.
Mary Lu is not a fan of grasshoppers,
especially when served
as hors d'oeuvre poppers.
Her sister, Lanore, detests
a mosquito biting her leg,
because she'll scratch all night
until Sara-Sara has to beg.
Jack doesn't like bats
and he knows that they're not an insect,
however, they are an intricate part
to the cause and the effect.
To sum it up, insects may be pests
and give pains with their bites,
but like every creature God has made,
they also have their rights.

November ❻

(Day 311 of 366)

Let's see what the Bible📖 has to say:

⚎ Matthew 3:4 John's clothes were made of camel's hair, and he had a leather belt around his waist. His food was locusts and wild honey.

When Kimberella finds herself worrying,
she remembers instead to pray.
Worrying can make a person sick,
but God can make any problem go away.

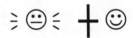

November ❼
(Day 312 of 366)

Let's see what the Bible📖 has to say:

✝ Matthew 6:27 "Who of you by worrying can add a single hour to his life?"

**Jack likes to have a positive attitude,
which is easy to do when you love the Lord.
He doesn't understand people who are a grouch
or walk around complaining when they are bored.
He knows enough to keep his distance
from those who rant and rave
and never wishes to get even with the world,
because that's not the way for a Christian to behave.**

November ❽

(Day 313 of 366)

Let's see what the Bible📖 has to say:

✝ **Proverbs 22:24** Do not make friends with a hot-tempered man, do not associate with one easily angered, for you may learn his ways and get yourself ensnared.

Baby No-No and Chew-Chew
are too little to know
that they won't go to Hell
if they don't use a pew every week for a perch.
Many people have that drilled
into their heads since birth,
but they really need to be born again
and *then* they *become* the Church.

✝ ♥

November ⑨

(Day 314 of 366)

Let's see what the Bible has to say:

✝ 1 Corinthians 12:27 Now you are the body of Christ, and each one of you is a part of it.

.

The Buckskin clan knows that there are anti-hunters who don't want to see an animal being killed for food. Buddy knows what would happen if it all stopped – all the vegetarians' crops would be chewed.

A vicious cycle...

November **10**
(Day 315 of 366)

Let's see what the Bible📖 has to say:

✝ Genesis 9:3 Everything that lives and moves will be food for you. Just as I gave you the green plants, I now give you everything.

**Today when Buddy read his Bible,
it talked about honor.
He cleaned up his living room
and had some other chores to do.
Then he called up his parents
to invite them for dinner,
because he is to honor his father
and his mother, too.**

November ❶❶

(Day 316 of 366)

Let's see what the Bible📖 has to say:

✝ Deuteronomy 5:16 Honor your father and your mother, as the Lord your God has commanded you, so that you may live long and that it may go well with you in the land the Lord your God is giving you.

If Fudgy and Witty Kitty were aboard Noah's ark,
they would have studied the sheep.
This would have been an impossible task,
since all the cat and dog do is sleep.
The sheep are called a ram, ewe or lamb
and are raised mainly for their fleece,
but they also provide much needed milk
to make our dreams be dreamt in peace.

≈≈≈◇≈≈≈

November ❶❷
(Day 317 of 366)

Let's see what the Bible has to say:

† John 10:11 "I am the good Shepherd. The good Shepherd lays down his life for the sheep."

D.J. has a problem,
but it's not what you think...
he doesn't stop what he's doing
to have a little drink.
His dilemma comes
when he looks out into the crowd
and sees others getting in fist fights
and yelling really loud.
He will turn up his guitar
and strum with his power
that will send the brawlers
under the tables to cower.
"Everything in moderation,"
is the message he'll relay,
"turn away from alcohol,
so you'll have a better day."

@(* - *)@

November ❶❸

(Day 318 of 366)

Let's see what the Bible📖 has to say:

✝ Proverbs 20:1 Wine is a mocker and beer a brawler; whoever is led astray by them is not wise.

Jules watched a chameleon turn different colors –
it was an amazing sight and very unexpected.
She was studying in the middle of a campus,
when along came a lizard that turned from green to red.
"You would be handy on my Christmas tree at home,"
she told the little fellow who was nibbling on her cheese,
"I have a string of lights that never work quite right."
He was hoping that this wasn't just some kind of tease.
As promised, Jules put the chameleon onto a light
and tied him with a string of popcorn around his back.
He ate his fill, balancing in place, trying to do his thing,
out of nowhere he changed colors, not red, but to black!
Once again, Jules could see that
he couldn't have evolved.
She knows that God designed the changing reptile.
He gave the lizard a way to be
protected from his enemies.
Maybe God made certain creatures
just to make us smile.

November ❶❹

(Day 319 of 366)

Let's see what the Bible📖 has to say:

✝ Genesis 1:31 God saw all that He had made, and it was very good. And there was evening, and there was morning – the sixth day.

Kimberella is a fantastic gardener!
It's *so* fantastic, it hard for K.T. to believe...
God is actually the Master Gardener –
He created every kind of plant for Adam and Eve.
Roots, trunks, branches, twigs,
stems, leaves, buds and seeds.
Grasses, veggies, cat tails, bushes,
soil, rain, sunshine and even weeds.

Everything!

November ❶❺

(Day 320 of 366)

Let's see what the Bible📖 has to say:

✝ **Genesis 1:11** Then God said, "Let the land produce vegetation: seed-bearing plants and trees on the land that bear fruit with seed in it, according to their various kinds. And it was so.

**The General wants to talk to you
about the difference between mercy and grace.
What he is about to tell you goes for everyone,
no matter what is your race:
"God's mercy is *not* giving you something
you *do* deserve, like death for your strife –
God's grace is *giving* you something
you *don't* deserve, like the gift of eternal life!"**

✝

November ❶❻

(Day 321 of 366)

Let's see what the Bible has to say:

⊤ Luke 6:36 Be merciful, just as your Father is merciful.
Romans 11:6 And if by grace, then it is no longer by works;
if it were, grace would no longer be grace.

Prince Roderick caught an octopus
while he was deep sea fishing.
Everyone was surprised to see
that its color was orange.
Kimberella was especially baffled
what to do with this information,
since she knows that orange
is an impossible word to rhyme (oh, brother!)
When they took the thingy off the hook
and put it on the floor,
it turned white, because the boat
was the color of an aspirin pill.
Mrs. Buckskin cried like a baby
when her brother-in-law insisted she tasted it,
'cause she doesn't eat black meat of any kind,
you see...it was cooked on a charcoal grill.

November ❶❼

(Day 322 of 366)

Let's see what the Bible📖 has to say:

† Romans 14:23 But the man who has doubts is condemned if he eats, because his eating is not from faith; and everything that does not come from faith is sin.

Sara-Sara was watching the news
to see what the forecast held for tomorrow.
By the time she turned off the television,
her happy mood turned into one of sorrow.
They predicted everything from hail and wind
to a possible tornado after just a few sprinkles.
If the sun popped out in the middle of it,
it would burn her skin and make more wrinkles.
She asked Jack, "What happened to rain showers
and a sunny day to hang your laundry out?"
He replied, "That wouldn't get people's attention
or give the politicians something to debate about."

✸ ☁ ▢

November ❶❽

(Day 323 of 366)

Let's see what the Bible has to say:

† Psalm 148:8 Lightning and hail, snow and clouds,
stormy winds that do His bidding.

**Mary Lu and Lanore
were in a play at their church.
The older of the two
lost her lines and went on a search.
Lanore decided to become
Jesus' mother for Mary Lu.
She said to the servants,
"Do whatever He tells you to."**

✝

November ❶❾

(Day 324 of 366)

Let's see what the Bible has to say:

☦ John 2:5 His mother said to the servants, "Do whatever He tells you."

**Mary Lu came up with this song
after attending Sunday School last weekend:**

**Saturday in the Ark –
every day is cloudy and gray.
Saturday in the Ark –
will it please dry up so I can play?
Animals eating, animals snoring –
a yearlong stay-cation...
How much can I take?**

**Saturday in the Ark –
I think the sky has turned a bright blue.
Another day in the Ark –
and then we can get outta this zoo.**

≈≈≈⌂≈≈≈

November ❷⓪
(Day 325 of 366)

Let's see what the Bible📖 has to say:

✝ Genesis 7:1 The Lord then said to Noah, "Go into the ark, you and your whole family, because I have found you righteous in this generation."

**Rochelle and Buddy were praying
inside a restaurant
and heard whispering,
making Rochelle's face like a rose.
Buddy told his friend
not to worry and wear it with pride,
because being called a Christian
means that it shows.**

☺ ✝ ☺

🍽 🍽

November ②①
(Day 326 of 366)

Let's see what the Bible has to say:

 1 Peter 4:16 However, if you suffer as a Christian, do not be ashamed, but praise God that you bear that name.

Baby No-No and her sister
were pretending they were princesses.
They gazed into the mirror before them
and saw their tiaras and puffy dresses.
Mommy passed by and saw them
and she recalled some verses from memory –
of crowns that are mentioned in the Bible
for beauty, life, righteousness and glory.

✝

November ❷❷

(Day 327 of 366)

Let's see what the Bible📖 has to say:

✝ James 1:12 Blessed is the man who perseveres under trial, because when he has stood the test, he will receive the crown of life that God has promised to those who love Him.

They think they figured out the Bermuda Triangle.
Well...then again, maybe they did not.
Air bombs or microbursts *could* be the cause
to make ships and planes on radar lose their dot.
Pilots and captains that survived an ordeal
say they saw on glass a slimy goo.
Some say the needles on instruments
went in circles or stopped as a clue.
Some things are just a mystery
and they may never be solved,
but there *is* a God who is Almighty
who *knows* what *exactly* is involved.
If you're sailing or flying from Florida
and need to head northeast,
Chew-Chew says to pray about taking the long way,
so you can enjoy another Thanksgiving Day's feast.

November ❷❸

(Day 328 of 366)

Let's see what the Bible📖 has to say:

✝ **1** Timothy 3:16 Beyond all question, the mystery of godliness is great: He appeared in a body, was vindicated by the Spirit, was seen by angels, was preached among the nations, was believed on in the World, was taken up in glory.

D.J. knows that when he wakes up in the morn',
he didn't improve from the night before.
If he doesn't touch his hair and leaves his home,
when he comes back in, it's still messy...even more.
If D.J. doesn't get out a pan to fry himself some eggs,
sits in a chair waiting for them to roll out of the fridge,
he'll have a better chance of getting something to eat
if he reaches with hands to catch fish from a bridge.
In other words, Evolution just doesn't work,
because *nothing* gets better with time,
unless it's a piece of fruit growing on a tree
and it turns from an unripe ball to a delicious lime.

☺ ☺ ☹ ☠

November ②④

(Day 329 of 366)

Let's see what the Bible📖 has to say:

✝ **Ezekiel 44:20 'They must not shave their heads or let their hair grow long, but they are to keep the hair of their heads trimmed.'**

Jack and Sara-Sara bought
Chia pets for their girls.
They spread the goop
and watched them turn green.
This made them think
about creating life in a lab...
it would prove *intelligence*,
not chance or a magic bean.

$$2 + 2 = 4$$

November ❷❺

(Day 330 of 366)

Let's see what the Bible📖 has to say:

✝ Proverbs 1:7 The fear of the Lord is the beginning of knowledge, but fools despise wisdom and discipline.

Sometimes Buddy suffers from burnout.
He will drag his feet, but keeps plugging along.
These are the times that he prays to God
to have delight and desire and praise Him with song.

♪ ♫

November ❷❻
(Day 331 of 366)

Let's see what the Bible📖 has to say:

† Psalm 37:4 Delight yourself in the Lord and He will give you the desires of your heart.

Witty Kitty tries to love his neighbor
by not giving them the "what for".
He also tries to forgive his enemies,
even down to the nasty biting fleas.
This isn't always easy to do for us –
it's much easier to throw them under the bus;
but God didn't say life would be one of ease,
so try to get along with your foes, won't you please?

November ❷❼

(Day 332 of 366)

Let's see what the Bible📖 has to say:

✝ Romans 12:20 On the contrary: "If your enemy is hungry, feed him; if he is thirsty, give him something to drink. In doing this, you will heap burning coals on his head."

Jesus died on the cross
over two thousand years ago
for each and everyone's sins...
D.J. hopes you know.
Our works don't save us,
but proves our faith in Jesus.
So get off of the
"Am I good enough?" bus!

✚

November ❷❽

(Day 333 of 366)

Let's see what the Bible📖 has to say:

✝ 2 Peter 3:9 The Lord is not slow in keeping His promise, as some understand slowness. He is patient with you, not wanting anyone to perish, but everyone to come to repentance.

Chew-Chew was learning his colors with his daddy:
"This is blue, this one's red and that one is yellow."
It didn't take long for the little tyke to figure it out,
because he was born an intelligent fellow.
They walked outside after the rain had stopped
and both looked up at the sky.
There, with seven different colors in all,
was a beautiful rainbow way up high.
The General took the time to explain to his son
that God put the rainbow there in its place
to be a colorful sign of the covenant
between The Almighty and the human race.

≈≈≈⌂≈≈≈

November ❷❾

(Day 334 of 366)

Let's see what the Bible📖 has to say:

✝ Genesis 9:12 "I have set my rainbow in the clouds, and it will be the sign of the covenant between me and the earth."

**Prince Roderick doesn't like to talk about fear,
but we all have to deal with it from time-to-time.
You should keep in mind to fear no one but God;
ask Him to fight for *you* if you've turned into a mime.**

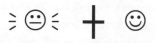

November ❸⓪
(Day 335 of 366)

Let's see what the Bible📖 has to say:

✝ 1 Corinthians 3:17 If anyone destroys God's temple, God will destroy him; for God's temple is sacred, and you are that temple.

Jules marvels at how the digestive system works
when she is at her desk as the coffee pot perks.
First she smells the freshly brewed coffee
and pours herself a cup to balance on her knee .
As she chews her donut and drinks out of her mug,
her taste buds are giving her mouth an inside hug.
She swallows the combo and yearns for more,
as her stomach is thanking her to the core.
Her body does its thing, going through the intestines,
after that, she'll leave it up to your imaginations.
The digestive system is just one of the many things
to live high on life without any wings.
Step-by-step each system was evolved?
Creation is the answer – this problem's solved!

√

December ❶

(Day 336 of 366)

Let's see what the Bible has to say:

⊤ Mark 7:19 For it doesn't go into his heart but into his stomach, and then out of his body.

Rochelle read that the sun is millions of miles away
and the light tracks all the way to us on Earth.
How then can one measly little cloud
block the sun like a planet with much more girth?

December ❷

(Day 337 of 366)

Let's see what the Bible📖 has to say:

✝ Ecclesiastes 1:5 The sun rises and the sun sets, and hurries back to where it rises.

**If Prince Roderick ever saw a Sasquatch,
he says he would never forget.
He would go to his grave defending his memory
of when the two of them met.
Kimberella knows that it wouldn't take long
to defend himself with others, that is.
Being scared silly would probably be quicker
than topping a cracker with Cheez Whiz!**

☠**R.I.P.**

December ❸
(Day 338 of 366)

Let's see what the Bible📖 has to say:

✝ Proverbs 19:2 It is not good to have zeal without knowledge, nor to be hasty and miss the way.

Izzy Ann gets asked quite often,
"Don't you know this or that?"
Being only five years old,
she can't think right off the bat.
When a teacher shows the girl
exactly what she means,
she slaps her cheek and gives a cry,
"I get it now...cool beans!"
Did it ever occur to *you*
that nothing occurs to God?
He knows what to do
from Heaven all the way down to *your* bod.

✝ I AM ✝

December ❹
(Day 339 of 366)

Let's see what the Bible has to say:

☩ Matthew 24:36 "No one knows about that day or hour, not even the angels in Heaven, nor the Son, but only the Father."

Lanore was chewing on her fingernails
and Sara-Sara asked her to stop.
"It can ruin your teeth biting like that
and you need them to open a soda pop."
Her daughter was confused at what her mommy said,
because she is never allowed to drink soda,
however, her friend, toothless Joey
manages to drink *his* daily quota.
Fingernails and toenails were designed for a reason –
to protect our digits with a shell.
They can be used to pick up small objects,
not just a place for dirt to dwell.

December ❺

(Day 340 of 366)

Let's see what the Bible📖 has to say:

✝ Daniel 5:5 Suddenly the fingers of a human hand appeared and wrote on the plaster of the wall, near the lampstand in the royal palace. The king watched the hand as it wrote.

Buddy was walking down a creek one day,
looking down to see which rocks to step on.
All of a sudden a lizard ran across his boot
and as quickly as it appeared, the critter was gone.
It reminded him of an article he read last week
about a reptile deciding to turn into a bird.
Whether or not *it* decided or Evolution was used,
in Buddy's mind, both of these theories are absurd!
A lizard has scales and a bird is full of feathers...
there are just too many things to list plus more.
The Geologic Column really messes things up
making people think birds came *after* the dinosaur.
In a flood, birds would be on top,
since they can fly and have hollow bones.
The dinosaurs who also lived with man,
would be on the bottom, just like heavy stones.
The next time you see a bird flying above you,
please know that God created it way back when.
He didn't start with a creature as big as a barn
and *then* have it change to the size of a wren!

December ❻
(Day 341 of 366)

Let's see what the Bible📖 has to say:

† Genesis 1:20 "And God said, "Let the water teem with living creatures, and let birds fly above the earth across the expanse of the sky.""

**Izzy Ann was picked up
by her mommy after Sunday School,
where every lesson
could be considered a "Golden Rule".
She learned you don't go to Heaven
just by doing a good deed.
Otherwise, Jesus made a huge mistake
by dying on the cross...there would be no need.**

December **7**

(Day 342 of 366)

Let's see what the Bible📖 has to say:

✝ Titus 3:5 He saved us, not because of righteous things we had done, but the cause of His mercy. He saved us through the washing of rebirth and renewal by the Holy Spirit.

Sara-Sara told the boys and girls sitting at their desks
that fruits and vegetables come in a variety of colors.
This didn't surprise too many of the little munchkins,
since they help in the gardens of
their fathers and mothers.
"But did you know," the teacher went on saying,
"that each color is different nutrient-wise?"
She might have well asked her students
their Grandma's middle name and Gramp's shoe size.
"The banana is considered a white fruit
and has many things that's good for all of us."
A boy exclaimed, "I thought a banana was yellow!"
She corrected, "That's the peel or
paint on a school bus."
"A carrot is orange and has Vitamin A."
"I know," said a girl, "They're good for your eyes."
"This may be so," said Sara-Sara, holding up an apple.
"These come in *many* colors…here comes the 'Whys?'"

Why???

December ❽
(Day 343 of 366)

Let's see what the Bible📖 has to say:

† **Genesis 1:29** Then God said, "I give you every seed-bearing plant on the face of the whole earth and every tree that has fruit with seed in it. They will be yours for food."

Today when **Kimberella** read her Bible,
it talked about discipline.
This is a sore subject,
since she's a grandmother of five.
She decided that a punishment
for not picking up toys when asked,
would be to only let them eat *two* cookies
(instead of *six*)...it's amazing she's still alive!

♥♥♥♥♥

December ❾

(Day 344 of 366)

Let's see what the Bible📖 has to say:

† Proverbs 29:17 Discipline your son; and he will give you peace; he will bring delight to your soul.

**Fudgy asked Witty Kitty,
"How much time do you think it would take
to have humans and animals evolve
after crawling out of the lake?"
Think about every last animal,
fish and insect that are on this earth
having to go through a process
in order to have what they need to give birth.
The only way possible
to imagine such an amazing feat
is to stir in millions and billions of years
over a *very* low heat.
Somehow everything is alright
to believe in *this* fairy tale
when minds try to wrap themselves
around it all and fail.
Fudgy asks that people unwash their brains
with a fool-proof soap
called reading the Bible
and give Evolution a great big:**

 *"NOPE!"*

✝ ⚵

December ❶⓪

(Day 345 of 366)

Let's see what the Bible📖 has to say:

✝ John 8:31 To the Jews who had believed Him, Jesus said, "If you hold to my teaching, you are really my disciples."

When Baby No-No was born,
the nurse rushed over to her crib.
There was serious business to be done,
like counting digits and putting on a bib.
God gave us fingers and toes
so we can do things and go places.
Holding her own bottle with her toes
will bring many smiles to her parents' faces.
Our fingers can play the piano,
unless you prefer the guitar.
Our toes gives us balance
and without them, we wouldn't travel far.
So count your blessings on your fingers
and wiggle your toes in the sand.
You can find these useful appendages
at the end of your foot and your hand.

December ❶❶

(Day 346 of 366)

Let's see what the Bible📖 has to say:

✝ Luke 1:44 As soon as the sound of your greeting reached my ears, the baby in my womb leaped for joy.

If Prince Roderick were aboard Noah's ark,
he would have studied the wolf.
Not because he's interested in the animal,
just to make Kimberella try to rhyme with it (UGH!)
The gray wolf is native to the wilderness
and the males can weigh up to one hundred pounds.
Their fur is long and bushy (and you guessed it, gray);
they eat small animals and trash, like coffee grounds.

≈≈≈◇≈≈≈

December ❶❷

(Day 347 of 366)

Let's see what the Bible📖 has to say:

✝ Luke 10:3 "Go! I am sending you out like lambs among wolves."

Chew-Chew is way too little to understand
what an appendix is *or* his right from his left hand.
Uncle Jack knows that the appendix can be taken out
and nobody would even think about giving a shout.
Who knows why this organ that God designed
isn't something that ever crosses our mind?
However, as for Chew-Chew and Uncle Jack,
they'll keep theirs *unless* there's an unexpected attack.

Don't touch! ✋

December ❶❸
(Day 348 of 366)

Let's see what the Bible📖 has to say:

† 3 John 1:2 Dear friend, I pray that you may enjoy good health and that all may go well with you, even as your soul is getting along well.

When Mary Lu went on a field trip,
she hopped on a bus to visit a pumpkin patch.
The ground she walked on was flat as a pancake –
if a tornado would have come, she'd go down a hatch.
Her pen pal, Inky, lives in Colorado
and wrote her class that she has to be on her toes,
'cause when Flood waters receded many moons ago,
the valleys sunk down and the mountains arose.

December ❶❹

(Day 349 of 366)

Let's see what the Bible📖 has to say:

† **Psalm 104:8** They flowed over the mountains, they went down into the valleys, to the place you assigned for them.

Lanore was playing with a top
on Grandpa's tiled floor.
She laughed and laughed until it stopped
and then she begged for more.
He tried to explain that the universe
used to run like a top,
because it was first going really fast
and is slowly coming to a stop.
No matter how fast and smooth
the toy starts out,
it's going to begin to wobble
and there is just no doubt.
Things don't get better with time
or even stay the same.
The top then fell over on the floor
and Lanore found herself a new game.

↰ ↱ ↳ ↵

December ❶❺

(Day 350 of 366)

Let's see what the Bible📖 has to say:

 Joshua 10:12 On the day the Lord gave the Amorites over to Israel, Joshua said to the Lord in the presence of Israel: "O sun, stand still over Gibeon, O moon, over the Valley of Aijalon."

Baby No-No gets into all kinds of trouble.
She likes to crawl where she doesn't belong.
Witty Kitty has very long whiskers used to rub with,
so *he* knows if the space is just right or just wrong.

December ❶❻

(Day 351 of 366)

Let's see what the Bible📖 has to say:

⊺ Psalm 34:10 The lions may grow weak and hungry, but those who seek the Lord lack no good thing.

Fudgy has a stubby tail,
but he wasn't born that way.
He had a long bushy one,
but he didn't have a say.
His owners before the Buckskins
wanted him to go short,
so they lobbed most of it off,
just like an unwanted wart.
God designed animals' tails,
so they have balance while running –
not 'cause they knock things over
wagging it while funning.
Some critters us it as a rudder
as they cross a river or brook.
You can tell a dog's emotional state
just like reading a child's book.
If they wag or wiggle it
from side to side really fast,
it means they are very happy
and you hope it can last.
If it's put between their legs
and their head is hanging low,
don't expect them to kiss you
on your cheek or even your big toe.

December ❶❼

(Day 352 of 366)

Let's see what the Bible📖 has to say:

✝ **Exodus 11:7** 'But among the Israelites not a dog will bark at any man or animal.' Then you will know that the Lord makes a distinction between Egypt and Israel.

**Kimberella gets her
financial statements monthly
from the local bank,
showing their investments.
They want her to go paperless
and visit their website
so *she* can print them off
and save *them* a few cents.**

December ❶❽

(Day 353 of 366)

Let's see what the Bible📖 has to say:

✝ Romans 15:4 For everything that was written in the past was written to teach us, so that through endurance and the encouragement of the Scriptures we might have hope.

Witty Kitty doesn't like water,
because it makes him climb up the walls.
So it might surprise you to hear
that he went in a barrel over the Falls.
He was on a trip out east
with his family of five that he loves.
The cat made his decision to try it
when he felt at peace while seeing some doves.
Jules and The General were on a mission
to study Niagara with all of its wonder.
Scientists say the Falls are shrinking,
but the math must be some kind of blunder.
If the world is *supposedly* billions of years old
and the Falls are shrinking back,
then they would be shrunk rearwards
from here to somewhere in Iraq.

December ❶❾

(Day 354 of 366)

Let's see what the Bible📖 has to say:

† Isaiah 43:2 When you pass through the rivers, they will not sweep over you. When you walk through the fire, you will not be burned; their flames will not set you ablaze.

Auntie K.T. turned to her Bible
to learn how to care for the earth.
She also was looking for
an exercise program to keep her fit.
The Book of Genesis says
that God took man and placed him
in the Garden of Eden,
so he can work and also help keep it.

December ❷⓪

(Day 355 of 366)

.

Let's see what the Bible has to say:

† Genesis 2:15 The Lord God took the man and put him in the Garden of Eden to work it and take care of it.

Jack was conducting a survey
when he was at a large job site.
He took notes watching his crew
drink coffee, sodas and eat chocolate bites.
Caffeine, for those who can tolerate it,
can be beneficial in keeping them alert,
but for the people who can't handle it,
it can mean a world of anxiety and hurt.

꒞ 😐 ꒦

December ❷❶

(Day 356 of 366)

Let's see what the Bible📖 has to say:

✝ **1** Peter 5:10 And the God of all grace, who called you to His eternal glory in Christ, after you have suffered a little while, will Himself restore you and make you strong, firm and steadfast.

**The reason Rochelle thinks others have a problem
with believing that there really is a Hell,
is because they want to keep living their lives
as if everything will turn out just swell.
When God says something, He really means it
and this you can be sure...
if He said He created a place like Heaven,
than you can *believe* Hell isn't just a blur.**

✝

December ❷❷

(Day 357 of 366)

Let's see what the Bible has to say:

† Matthew 25:46 "Then they will go away to eternal punishment, but the righteous to eternal life."

Sara-Sara had her class go on a field trip
to Kentucky, which from Iowa is quite a ways.
She wanted them to experience the "Ark Encounter"
to see the four story structure that would amaze.
When they were back in school the next Monday,
she had her students make out a family tree.
They all put Noah at the top of the page,
since everyone is a descendent of him, you see.

December ②③

(Day 358 of 366)

Let's see what the Bible📖 has to say:

✝ Acts 17:26 From one man He made every nation of men, that they should inhabit the whole earth; and He determined the times set for them and the exact places where they should live.

Jack doesn't appreciate being called an ape,
but then again, who would?
Sometimes his co-workers tease and poke fun,
instead of working like they really should.
All humans are made in God's image,
which separates us from a furry beast.
He also gave us the power to talk,
so maybe an *apology* could be in order, at least?

Forgiveness

December **24**

(Day 359 of 366)

Let's see what the Bible has to say:

Ephesians 5:4 Nor should there be obscenity, foolish talk or coarse joking, which are out of place, but rather thanksgiving.

**Izzy Ann is only five years old,
but she still can understand quite a bit.
Taking Christ out of Christmas is a lot like
taking the Creator out of Creation...*Oh*... that's it!**

$$X \neq \dagger$$

December ❷❺

(Day 360 of 366)

Let's see what the Bible📖 has to say:

✝ John 3:18 Whoever believes in Him is not condemned, but whoever does not believe stands condemned already because he has not believed in the name of God's one and only Son.

D.J. decided to put down his guitar
and climbed to his garage roof instead.
He thought stargazing would be more exciting
than tossing and turning all night in his bed.
After D.J. looked through his telescope
and saw many wondrous stars,
he whipped out his trusty notepad
and made up a song to be played in cars.
He wrote that God created the lesser light
after He created the light for the day.
The stars including the constellations
are dimmer, but light enough to find our way.
So next time when you're on your porch
and see the patterns of stars across the sky,
give thanks to God who took the time
just for you to enjoy while eating a slice of pie.

★ ☆ ★ ☆ ★ ☆

December ❷❻
(Day 361 of 366)

Let's see what the Bible has to say:

⊤ Psalm 19:1 The heavens declare the glory of God; the skies proclaim the work of His hands.

**Fudgy turned to his Bible
to learn about sanitation
after hearing the neighbor's
and the Buckskins' argument.
The Book of Deuteronomy says
to have a certain tool with you,
so after relieving yourself,
you dig a hole to cover your excrement.**

(In Fudgy's case, he *could* have used his paws)

I can dig it!

December ❷❼

(Day 362 of 366)

Let's see what the Bible📖 has to say:

✝ Deuteronomy 23:13 As part of your equipment have something to dig with, and when you relieve yourself, dig a hole and cover up your excrement.

The General,
along with his wife, Jules,
like to cruise in their car,
but also follow the rules.
They read all of the signs
along the road as they drive,
so they are safe and sound
when they finally arrive.
God wrote us a book
to use for our lives every day –
when you are in His Word,
it's hard to lose your way.
If you choose to go on another path
that seems a little faster,
please make a U-turn,
so *instead* you obey God, your Master.

December ❷❽

(Day 363 of 366)

Let's see what the Bible📖 has to say:

✝ Hebrews 4:12 For the word of God is living and active. Sharper than any double-edged sword, it penetrates even to dividing soul and spirit, joints and marrow; it judges the thoughts and attitudes of the heart.

**Kimberella says that God will never leave.
He'll never give up and is always there to guide.
He started something in you and will see you through
from the beginning to the end...He is on your side.**

♥♥ Go Team! 🏆 🏅

December ❷❾
(Day 364 of 366)

Let's see what the Bible has to say:

✝ Philippians 4:13 I can do everything through Him who gives me strength.

"Baby No-No don't know nothin',"
Prince Roderick, her grandpa will say.
His wife will cringe whenever she hears it,
just like she did when she heard it today.
How can *anyone* believe that we evolved
and to top it off, we could reproduce?
Don't think only of a human baby,
but everything from a mouse to a moose.
Come on people! Let's get real!
God deserves all of the credit for sure!
A baby is just *one* of His wondrous miracles,
whether the baby is born a him or a her.

December **30**

(Day 365 of 366)

Let's see what the Bible📖 has to say:

✝ Job 31:15 Did not He who made me in the womb make them? Did not the same One form us both within our mothers?

Sara-Sara is not a homebody,
but she hasn't been to the West Indies.
She has a level head about things
and doesn't rush into chasing fantasies.
This doesn't just mean going on trips,
visiting people and maybe sightsee –
God means not to live in La-La-Land,
but grow some solid roots like a tree.

December ❸❶

(Day 366 of 366)

Let's see what the Bible📖 has to say:

✝ Proverbs 28:19 He who works his land will have abundant food, but the one eager to get rich will not go unpunished.